Rectors and Clergy of H

Rectors and Clergy

of the Parish of

St Margaret of Antioch

Hemingford Abbots

BY

CHARLES BERESFORD AND DAVID YEANDLE

Contents

Illustrations

Abbreviations

CCEd   Clergy of the Church of England Database (1540–1835)

C of E   Church of England, also known as the Anglican Church

ODNB Oxford Dictionary of National Biography

PCC   Parochial Church Council

RCHM Royal Commission on Historical Monuments

Acknowledgements

Photographs of St Margaret's by Manuela Yeandle are used by kind permission.

We wish to acknowledge with thanks the generous support of the Goodliff Fund of the Huntingdon Local History Society for a grant to enable the publication of this book.

We are grateful to Dr Anthony Bowen, Simon Clemmow, Bridget Flanagan, Alan Richardson, Richard Selwyn Sharpe, and several other friends for their encouragement and for sharing their expertise.

Preface

The aim of the book is to provide a historical overview of the parish of Hemingford Abbots through the details of the individual clergy who have had responsibility for the 'cure of souls' over the centuries. The patrons, who influenced their appointment, and the church building, where they led worship, are integral to most of their stories.

A prelude about the present village precedes a summary of the historical context of its church. We then focus on the clergy.

Details of the rectors, curates, and patrons since the Reformation are listed in the chronological order of their appointment. Inevitably, much more is known or remembered about some than others.

Many of the clergy served other parishes as well. In the past, some received income from several parishes in plurality. Indeed, it is possible that some incumbents never set foot in the parish.

Little is known about the curates, non-stipendiary ministers, retired clergy, lay readers, licensed lay ministers, and visiting clergy, who were often significant, both in preaching and helping the rector or priest-in-charge with pastoral duties.

The sections about the rectors between Henry Herbert and David Young (1867–1977), on pp. 97–147, were serialized in the Hemingford Abbots *Parish Magazine* in 2020–21.

Lists of clergy, in date and name order, are to be found in the Appendix (pp. 171–177), together with their number in the Clergy of the Church of England Database (CCEd), where appropriate.

The authors would be grateful for any corrections or comments.

Please send these by email to:
charlesberesford24@gmail.com
or davidnyeandle@gmail.com

The Parish of St Margaret

Continuity

The twelfth-century font pictured below has been used by the clergy described in this book to baptize parishioners and their relatives for many centuries.

Figure 1 The Font

The font also emphasizes the passage of time. The octagonal shape of the font, its four octagonal columns, and its cylindrical shaft together represented resurrection and new life. 'Frequently an arcade in relief, imitating closely the structural arcade of the period, adorns a Norman font … The ornamental arcading of round arches testifies to the early date, as at Hemingford Abbots and St Ives (Hunts), Langham (Norfolk) and Bosham (Sussex).'[1] The evidence of partial restoration is a reminder that, for a time, it was considered too primitive and was used in a farmyard before being restored in the nineteenth century.

The Peace window in the south aisle symbolizes the outward-looking ethos of applying Christian values in everyday life. The quotation 'the Peace of God that passeth all understanding' was engraved by a parishioner, and it can stimulate a reminder that the church building and its surroundings are peaceful places for worship and reflection.

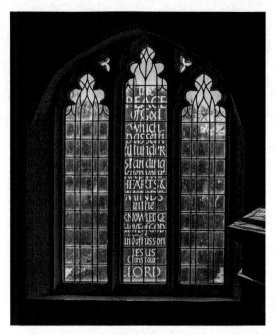

Figure 2 Peace window

[1] E. Tyrrell-Green, *Baptismal Fonts: Classified and Illustrated*, Historic Monuments of England (London: New York: Society for Promoting Christian Knowledge; Macmillan Co., 1928), pp. 29, 76.

Community

The village of Hemingford Abbots today is a quiet settlement in a conservation area along the south bank of the southern arm of the Great Ouse.[2] At this point, it divides into two around a large tract of meadowland before reuniting with the northern branch, shortly before reaching Hemingford Grey. It lies approximately half-way between river crossings at the Roman road hub of Godmanchester and at St Ives, with its medieval bridge and chapel on the pilgrim route to Ramsey Abbey. Although the main settlement follows the course of the river, the 2,421 acres (979.7 hectares) of the parish extend southwards over mainly arable land. It crosses the A1307, formerly the Roman Via Devana, until it meets the A1198, formerly the Roman Ermine Street.

The population in 2020 was estimated at 634.[3] In 1841, the population peaked at 564, but had declined to 296 by 1931. The village includes forty-four listed buildings as well as what Pevsner in 1968 somewhat uncharitably called 'a recent rash of small private houses'.[4] By the twenty-first century, many of these houses had either been demolished and replaced by sizeable dwellings on the generous plots of land or had been extended significantly to suit the requirements of the changing population. Whereas the village was formerly devoted to agriculture, it has developed into a dormitory community for commuters to surrounding towns and cities, including London. Whereas in the 1950s to 1970s, several inhabitants were professionals or ex-military personnel, in the twenty-first century, more are engaged in business and commerce, with a higher income. The high price of housing in what some estate agents have referred to as 'Huntingdonshire's premier village' has led to an aging, prosperous population, 42% of whom are over 60.[5]

[2] See 'The Hemingfords Conservation Area June 2008 Character Assessment', https://www.huntingdonshire.gov.uk/media/2326/hemingfords-ca-character-assessment-adopted-june-2008.pdf.

[3] See 'City Population', https://www.citypopulation.de/en/uk/eastofengland/admin /huntingdonshire/E04012026__hemingford_abbots/.

[4] Nikolaus Pevsner, *The Buildings of England: Bedfordshire and the County of Huntingdon and Peterborough* (Harmondsworth: Penguin Books, 1968), p. 261.

[5] https://www.citypopulation.de/en/uk/eastofengland/admin/huntingdonshire /E04012026__hemingford_abbots/.

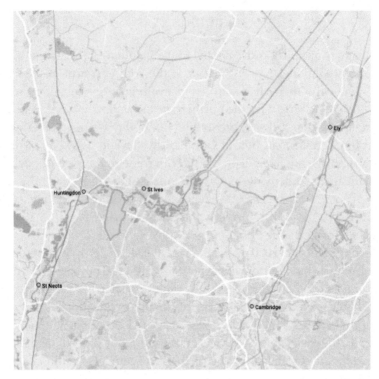

Figure 3 Parish boundary and location

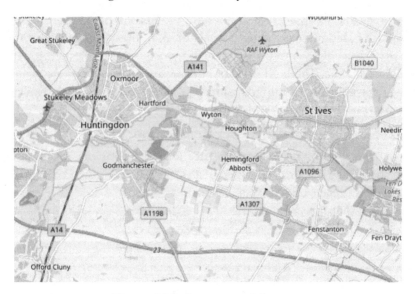

Figure 4 Modern map of the area

The village has little by way of commerce, no shops, no longer a school, so the focus of community life is on the pub, the village hall, and the church. The church is in the fortunate position of attracting significant support from the whole village for the biennial flower festivals. A considerable proportion of the community is involved in collaborating to welcome thousands of visitors over a weekend in June. They come to see a floral exhibition in the church, side shows and exhibitions, and a range of gardens in the village. Substantial funds are raised for the improvement and maintenance of the church building, which, unlike many village churches, is kept well maintained and tastefully decorated.[6]

Figure 5 St Margaret's church decorated for a flower festival

The flower festivals keep the church as a focus of village life in a way that it might not otherwise be. Its influence has, in common with national trends, steadily declined since the 1950s, but its style of worship and strong musical tradition have ensured a steady congregation and choir, drawn from the parish and further afield.

Worship at St Margaret's is noteworthy for its musical tradition, which extends well back into the twentieth century. A succession of organists, choirmasters, and singers with choral experience of the rich

[6] https://hemingfordabbots.org.uk/.

collegiate and cathedral tradition of Anglican music has ensured that a musical offering of a type usually found in a much larger church has continued to enrich the worship at St Margaret's. Mention might especially be made of Miss Grace Unwin, who was organist for many years until 1994 and whose efforts and abilities laid a firm foundation for choral worship in the church, which has been supported by several incumbents.

Patronage of the living by the Herbert family has ensured that moderate, middle-of-the-road clergy were appointed to the living, and they continued the traditions established over 150 years ago. Since 1989, the situation has been more fluid, reflecting the need to share resources with other parishes, but essentially, the church has upheld a broad-church style of worship, typical of traditional Anglicanism.

Figure 6 Roman sarcophagus, c. 300 AD

The Context

Two thousand years ago, the alluvial soils of the Ouse valley between Huntingdon and St Ives lay between the heavier clay to the north-west and south, and the fens to the north-east. River crossings, fertile soil, and good pasture had been attractive to settlement for centuries. Traces of a Neolithic camp floor at the west end of the village date from about 6000 BC,[7] and there is evidence of metalworking at the south Lattenbury end from around 2000 BC, which may have been contemporaneous with the causewayed enclosures and the massive trapezoidal enclosure at Rectory Farm, Godmanchester, which covered 6.3 hectares but is now covered by 20th-century waste disposal.[8]

In the first century, the Roman forts were linked by roads converging at Godmanchester (Durovigutum), south of the crossing of the River Ouse; at Alconbury, on the clay uplands; and at Water Newton (Durobrivae), near Peterborough, south of the crossing of the River Nene. Ermine Street came through Godmanchester on the route from London, going north to Peterborough, Lincoln, and York. Hemingford Abbots was the last settlement near the Via Devana from Cambridge before it reached Godmanchester.

The British Museum displays Christian silver objects found at Water Newton, dating from the late third century. This indicates that Christianity had arrived in the area before Constantine's Edict of Milan accepted it in 313. Ten years later, Christianity was adopted as the official religion of the previously polytheistic empire. Augustine's mission to Britain was in 597, and Peterborough's Benedictine monastery was founded in 655, followed by Ely's abbey in 673. They were later destroyed by the Danes and eventually restored: Peterborough in 963–66 and Ely in 972. Ramsey Abbey was founded in 969, and five years later was endowed with lands, including Hemingford Abbots.

[7] Cf. Tim Malim, 'Neolithic Enclosures', no. 8, in: Tony Kirby and Susan Oosthuizen, *An Atlas of Cambridgeshire and Huntingdonshire History* (Cambridge: Centre for Regional Studies, Anglia Polytechnic University, 2000).

[8] Alice Lyons, *EAA 170: Rectory Farm, Godmanchester, Cambridgeshire: Excavations 1988–95, Neolithic Monument to Roman Villa Farm* (Cambridge: East Anglian Archaeology, 2020).

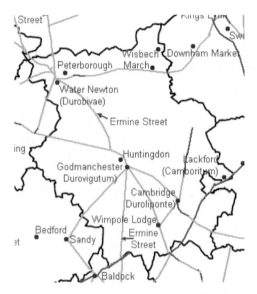

Figure 7 Roman roads in Cambridgeshire[9]

In Roman times there had been a villa near Ridgeway Farm on Ridea-way. A sarcophagus (stone tomb) was found in the nineteenth century in the adjacent field that belonged to the Lord of the Manor, Colonel Douglas, on the west side of Rideaway and brought to the church. At the same time, the font was found in a farmyard, where it was being used as a drinking trough for cattle.[10]

[9]   https://romanobritain.org/7-maps/map_counties_roads_towns _cambridgeshire.php.

[10] Madeline Herbert (widow of the Rev. Francis Herbert), communication to Lord Hemingford, 23 October 1977 (See Figure Figure 1, above). The same fate had befallen the much cruder, possibly Saxon, font of nearby Kimbolton church, which was being used as a drinking trough for cattle in Little Stukeley and was erected in St Andrew's church in 1918. http://standrew-kimbol-ton.org.uk/Guide.htm.

Hemingford Abbots Name

The people living in this area were a mixture of Romano-British and Anglo-Saxon ethnicity. The name Hemingford is of Germanic origin.[11] It is first attested, c. 975, in the form *Hemminggeford*, in a reference to a land claim in the *Liber Eliensis*, in which reference is made to King Edgar's death.[12] Edgar died on 8 July 975, so it may be assumed that the form of the name *Hemminggeford* goes back to this period, even though the *Liber Eliensis* was not written until the early twelfth century.[13] In the *Domesday Book* in 1086, the name is recorded as *Emingeford*. It is made up of three elements *Hem+ing+ford*. The first refers to an Anglo-Saxon name *Hemma* (or *Hemmi*). The *-ing-* element goes back to Old English *-inga-* or *-ingas*,

[11] '*Hemmingeford* 974, *Emingeford* 1086 (*db*), *Hemingford Abbatis* 1276, *Hemingford Grey* 1316. "Ford of the family or followers of a man called Hemma or Hemmi". OE pers. name + *inga* + *ford*. Distinguishing affixes from early possession by the Abbot of Ramsey and the *de Grey* family.' (Mills, 2011). See also Tony Kirby and Susan Oosthuizen, eds., *An Atlas of Cambridgeshire and Huntingdonshire History* (Cambridge: Centre for Regional Studies, Anglia Polytechnic University, 2000), p. 26 'Placenames 650—950 AD'.

[12] 'Postea vero, mortuo rege Ædgaro, filii cujusdam viri nomine Boge de Hemminggeford calumpniati sunt eandem terram, scilicet Bluntesham, dicentes, quod avunculus eorum, Tope vocabulo dictus, illam terram jure haereditario possidere deberet.' Thomas of Ely, supposed author Richard of Ely, and David James Stewart, *Liber Eliensis, ad fidem codicum variorum* (Londini, Impensis Societatis, 1848) http://archive.org/details/libereliensisadf01thom, p. 138. 'But afterwards, when King Edgar died [July 975], the sons of a man called Boga of Hemingford laid claim to that land at Bluntisham, saying that their uncle, called Tope, ought to have the land by right of inheritance.' Janet Fairweather, trans., *Liber Eliensis: A History of the Isle of Ely from the Seventh Century to the Twelfth* (Woodbridge: The Boydell press, 2005), Book II, Section 25, p. 121.

[13] Cf. 'Early through second-quarter 12th century' https://en.wikipedia.org /wiki/Liber_Eliensis.

which denotes a place connected to a preceding name;[14] *ford* denotes, as in modern English, a river crossing. It is unknown who Hemma was, though it has been suggested he may have been a Saxon chieftain. Thus, the name means 'ford of the people of Hemma or Hemmi'.[15] The Abbots element indicates its ownership by the Abbots of Ramsey, which was one of the richest monasteries in medieval England. The earliest reference to 'abbots' is in 1276: *Hemmyngford Abbatis* 'Hemingford of the Abbot', in the *Rotuli Hundredorum*. Other names for the village are: *West Hemyngford*, 1248; *Hemyngford Magna* ('Great Hemingford'), 1252; *Hemmyngeford iuxta Huntedon* ('Hemingford by Huntingdon'), 1286.[16]

After the Romans left the area, the Roman road and buildings were raided for their building materials. The area was near the boundary between two of the great Anglo-Saxon kingdoms, East Anglia and Mercia. The fens had become waterlogged again, and settlement was on the higher ground.

The rivers made the area vulnerable to attack by the Danes. In 870, they burnt the monastery at Ely and the abbey at Medeshamstede (Peterborough), slaughtering the monks. St Edmund, King of East Anglia, was also killed during this time. Some seized the part of Hemingford Grey north of the Roman road and settled in the area of the Thorpe. A century later, the times were more peaceful. King Edgar, Dunstan, Archbishop of Canterbury, and particularly Aethelwold, Bishop of Winchester, inspired the rebuilding of Ely and Medeshamstede.

[14] John McNeal Dodgson, 'The Significance of the Distribution of the English Place-Name in *-ingas, -inga-* in South-East England', *Medieval Archaeology*, 10.1 (1966), 1–29 https://doi.org/10.1080/00766097.1966.11735279.

[15] Cf. 'Both names are recorded in LVD [Liber Vitae of Durham], and in ultimate origin are probably short forms of some compound name in Hæm-, such as Hæmgils (cf. Bledda from Blæd-).' Survey of English Place-Names http://epns.nottingham.ac.uk/browse/Huntingdonshire/Hemingford+Abbots +and+Grey/53282b41b47fc407a900035d-Hemingford.

[16] *Ibid.*

The First Five Centuries

Ailwin or Æthelwine (d. 992) was Ealdorman of East Anglia.[17] He was a cousin of Edgar, King of Wessex from 959 until his death in 975.[18] Edgar was formally recognized as King of England and crowned in Bath in 973. Butterfield notes how 'Ailwin suffered cruelly from gout in both legs until he was suddenly cured—miraculously, as he believed—on Ram's Island (Ramsey), which then looked out over the marshes of the Fens. As a result of this cure, he resolved to build an abbey on that site as a thanksgiving, and construction began in the year 969, St Oswald, Archbishop of York, joining him as co-founder.'[19]

As the work on Ramsey Abbey progressed, Ailwin and Oswald made extensive donations of land for the Abbey's support.[20] Among Ailwin's gifts, was one of thirty hides of fertile land at Hemingford, together with provision for a church to be built there. A hide was a measure of land,

[17] An Ealdorman in the tenth century was a man of high status, who was the king's representative and a semi-independent ruler of a region such as East Anglia. The term evolved into that of 'Eorl' and then 'Earl'. The word 'ealdorman' survives as 'alderman', but the role is fundamentally different, being applied to senior members of some municipal councils.

[18] The name is spelled Ailwin, Aylwin, or Æthelwine in contemporary documents. Cf. J. Wise and W. M. Noble, *Ramsey Abbey: Its Rise and Fall* (Huntingdon: Edis & Cooper; Ramsey: Palmer & Son; London: Simpkin, Marshall & Co., 1881) https://books.google.co.uk/books?id=OQ0HAAAAQAAJ, p. 19.

[19] Richard Butterfield, 'All Aboard the Time Machine for a Thousand-Year Trip', *Hunts Post*, 2 May 1974, p. 4. In detail, see Wise and Noble, p. 44; https://en.wikipedia.org/wiki/Ramsey_Abbey.

[20] For a full description of the abbey's benefactors see *Liber benefactorum* of Ramsey Abbey (Susan Edgington, trans., *Ramsey Abbey's book of benefactors*, Great Britain: Hakedes, 2001). This was compiled in the mid-twelfth century, incorporating much valuable information on the early history of Ramsey and complementing material from other fenland houses. Pt I provides a twelfth-century view of the historical background (1998); Part II covers the period from the foundation of Ramsey to the deaths of Ealdorman Æthelwine and Bishop Oswald in 992 (2001); Part III will cover the period from 992 to 1066; and Part IV will cover the period after the Conquest.

based not upon area, as is the acre, but upon its productive capacity.[21] In this case, thirty hides were probably roughly equivalent to the 2421 acres of the existing parish of Hemingford Abbots and did not include the Danish area of Hemingford Grey north of the Roman road. That area was subsequently presented to the Abbey in either 1041 or 1042 by King Canute's son, Hardecanute, and widow, Emma of Normandy, before the return of the house of Wessex and Edward the Confessor.

When work on Ramsey's monastic buildings had been completed, King Edgar granted a charter to the Abbey. The year was 974, and this charter contained confirmation of gifts of land to the new foundation. It is, as far as we know, the first documentary record of Hemingford Abbots, though it is judged by modern scholarship to be untrustworthy in its present form.[22] Ailwyn's gift is commemorated on the tower screen of the church in an engraving in the glass by former parishioner Dr David Peace,[23] who commented, '… this particular in situ work is not easily visible except usually to those prepared to walk around to get the

---

[21] 'The number of virgates to the hide or acres to the virgate was increased or decreased until the territorial and fiscal hides agreed. Although, therefore, the average number of acres to the hide for all Ramsey manors was very little over 120, yet the variation in individual cases was very great.' (Nellie Neilson, 'Economic Conditions on the Manors of Ramsey Abbey', PhD Dissertation, Bryn Mawr College, Philadelphia, 1898 (Philadelphia: Sherman & Co., 1899), p. 13.

[22] 'This charter cannot, however, be trusted implicitly, as it has been much tampered with, if it be not, indeed, a forgery entirely.' Sawyer, P. H., *Anglo-Saxon Charters* (London: Royal Historical Society, 1968), p. 82.

[23] David Peace MBE, FSA, Hon. DSc (Tech.), Sheffield (1915–2003) was President of the Guild of Glass Engravers. He had specialized in conservation and environmental planning with Staffordshire and Cambridgeshire County Councils. There are thirty-three examples of his glass engraving in public collections, seventy-three windows, screens, and doors in public and private buildings and eleven other items of church glass, as well as seventy-two commissions for special occasions. The panel in the tower screen, commemorating him, was engraved in 2004 by his collaborator and co-author Sally Scott. 'Peace, David Brian, (13 March 1915–15 Feb. 2003), Glass Engraver; Town Planner, 1947–82', 2007. *Who's Who 2021* https://doi.org/10.1093/ww/9780199540884.013.U30334.

words against a dark background—a "kinetic" experience. Not all can wait till a summer evening with a western sun.'[24]

Figure 8 Millennium window (sketch)

By a thousand years ago, there were several cottages and a wooden church at Hemingford Abbots that had been built about fifty years earlier. The land would have been sufficient to maintain about thirty families with three acres each. In 1086, the *Domesday Book* recorded thirty-one property owners among the 150 residents.[25]

   Butterfield notes, 'To satisfy the land-hunger of his followers, William the Conqueror had to dispossess not only Saxon landowners but

[24] David Peace, *The Engraved Glass of David Peace: The Architecture of Lettering* (Sheffield: Ruskin Gallery: Sheffield City Arts Department,1990), p. 26.
[25] See Appendix, p. 169.

also the monasteries, although these still retained considerable holdings. The Hemingford which was to become "Abbots" continued in the ownership of Ramsey Abbey, but much of "the Other", or Grey, was grabbed by Aubrey de Vere shortly after 1077 and thereafter remained a secular manor.'[26]

In 1086, the *Domesday Book* provided details of the Abbey's landholdings and some of the challenges to their ownership. It also recorded that Ely was the second richest and Ramsey the fourth richest monastery in England at the time.

The Norman reorganisation of the dioceses to transfer bishops' sees from small to large towns led to Lincoln replacing Dorchester and the appointment of Remigius as bishop there in 1067. The bishopric of Ely was established in 1109, but Ramsey Abbey and Hemingford Abbots continued to be in Lincoln diocese until 1837, when Huntingdonshire was transferred to Ely.

---

[26] Butterfield, *ibid*.

Personnel and Estate

Figure 9 Village sign with the arms of Ramsey Abbey

Hemingford Abbots was linked with Ramsey Abbey from 974 until its dissolution by Henry VIII in 1537. During these five centuries, the Abbots of Ramsey appointed a succession of monks to care for the souls of the parishioners of Hemingford Abbots.[27] The abbey boosted St Ives as a riverport and market town by erecting a wooden bridge over the river Ouse in 1107. A charter for an Easter fair at St Ives was granted in 1110, and the abbey granted the church of Hemingford Abbots to St Ives Priory from 1131 to 1209. The Priory burnt down in 1207, and Hemingford Abbots reverted to the Abbey. In 1206, Abbot Robert of Reading resigned and was then maintained by the Manor of Cranfield, which had been given to the Abbey in 918. The Archbishop of Canterbury appointed three monks to be the receivers of the revenues of the Abbey.

[27] See Appendix, pp. 171–172.

King John held the Abbey for seven years without an abbot, because the monks would not choose the Prior of Fronton in south-west France as their abbot. In 1214, the appointment of Richard, Abbot of Selby, was procured by the Papal Legate Nicholas, but Richard died after two years.[28]

The first abbot is recorded as Ædnoth the younger (992–1008); the last was John Lawrence alias Wardeboys. A slab in the floor of St Margaret's chancel is reputed to be the tombstone of the last Abbot. Lombardic capitals around its edge contain the remains of an inscription in French: '. . . . [perso]ne: de: le: eglise: de [h]emyn[gf]ord . . . .'[29] In 1911, Mr E. L. Watts told Inskip Ladds that it had long been cast by the roadside and was brought to the churchyard by the Rev. Henry Herbert.[30]

Figure 10 Inscription in the chancel to a 'parson of Hemingford'

[28] Wise and Noble, pp. 119f.

[29] 'parson of Hemingford church'. See 'Parishes: Hemingford Abbots,' in *A History of the County of Huntingdon: Volume 2*, ed. William Page, Granville Proby and S Inskip Ladds (London: Victoria County History, 1932), 304–09. *British History Online*, http://www.british-history.ac.uk/vch/hunts/vol2/pp304-309.

[30] Inskip Ladds Archive, 'Hemingford Abbots', file 31 in the Norris Museum, St Ives.

Advowsons, Patrons, and Presentations

Figure 11 Abbot Ædnoth[31]

The earliest patrons[32] were the Abbots and monks of Ramsey, who supplied the first priests of Hemingford Abbots from amongst their ranks. Ramsey Abbey was the patron of eighteen churches and attached chapels and St Ives fair. These were confirmed by Pope Alexander III in 1178.[33] There are no records of named priests before one 'Aristotle', the dates of whom are uncertain, but his name is attested in documents of the late twelfth and early thirteenth century.[34] Clay has determined this

---

[31] Miniature of a bishop and an abbot from the 14th-century Ramsey Psalter, thought to be Oswald (left) and his kinsman Ædnoth (right), https://en.wikipedia.org/wiki/Eadnoth_the_Younger.

[32] Colin Alexander Weale, 'Patronage Priest and Parish in the Archdeaconry of Huntingdon 1109-1547' (PhD thesis, Middlesex University, 1996) https://eprints.mdx .ac.uk/13500/, pp. 66f.

[33] William Henry Hart and Ponsonby A. Lyons, eds., *Cartularium Monasterii de Rameseia*, Cambridge Library Collection - Rolls (Cambridge: Cambridge University Press, 2012), II https://doi.org/10.1017/CBO9781139380614, para. 357.

[34] See Charles Clay, 'Master Aristotle', *English Historical Review*, 76, No. 299 (April 1961), 303–08.

was master Aristotiles de Stukely, grandson of Henry, Archdeacon of Huntingdon, and a king's bailiff. The abbot who ruled when Aristotle was probably appointed to Hemingford Abbots was Robert Trianel (elected 1180, died 1200). The last priests to be appointed by the Abbey before the Reformation were Lewes Williams in 1513 and John London in 1524.[35]

The Monarch became the Head of the Church of England in February 1531. Pope Clement VII excommunicated Henry VIII in July 1533, and in August 1534, the Act of Supremacy marked the final severance of the Church in England from Rome. Five months later, the English bishops abjured papal authority, and the visitation of English churches and monasteries was ordered.

The two archbishops led the hierarchy of diocesan bishops, archdeacons, and parish priests. The appointment of an incumbent to serve God and the people of each parish became part of the secular role of the 'patron'. This right and responsibility was known as the advowson.[36]

The advowson was exercised mainly by the lords of the manor or directly by the Crown from 1537 to 1703.[37] The first presentation after the Dissolution (1536–41) was made 'pro hac vice'[38] by John Wiseman [Wyseman], a Member of Parliament from Canfield in Essex and one of Henry VIII's auditors, who presented Percival Lego to the living in 1544.[39] The presentation was made by grant from the dissolved abbey of Ramsey.[40]

The advowson of Hemingford Abbots had passed to the King's servant Oliver Leader, who sold it to Fotheringhay College in 1545. This was suppressed soon afterwards, and the Manor passed to the Duke of

---

[35] For details of the pre-Reformation presentations, see the table Pre-Reformation Clergy, Appendix, 171f.

[36] Cf. https://en.wikipedia.org/wiki/Advowson. Cf. https://www.british-history .ac.uk/vch/hunts/vol2/pp304-309.

[37] On the lordship of the manor after the Dissolution, see Page, Proby and Ladds, pp. 304–09.

[38] The meaning is 'for this turn', i.e. that the presentation was made by someone who was not the patron but had the right of presentation temporarily.

[39] See https://www.historyofparliamentonline.org/volume/1509-1558/member/ wiseman-john-1515-58.

[40] See CCEd 39968.

Northumberland. It was then granted to Sir Thomas Seymour, before his attainder and execution in 1549, when it reverted to the Crown.

Figure 12 Monumental brass to John and Agnes Wyseman[41]

The next two rectors, Thomas Thompson (1555) and Arthur Yeldard (1556) were presented by the Crown (Queen Mary I).

In 1574, Queen Elizabeth granted to Helen, Marchioness of Northampton,[42] for her lifetime, the Manors of St Ives, Hemingford Abbots, and Hemingford Grey.

[41] In St Mary's Church, Great Canfield, Essex: 'Here lyeth Jhon Wyseman esquire sutyme one of ye Audytors of ye Sovaign Lorde Kynge Henry the eight of ye Revenues of his crown & Agnes his wyfe, wch Jhon dyed ye xvij daye of August An Dm 1558 et annis regnarii Phillipi et Marie quinto et sept m' https://www.flickr.com/photos/norfolkodyssey/14151772955.

[42] Helen, née Snakenborg, came from Sweden at the age of 15 in the suite of the pregnant Princess Cecilia, daughter of King Gustavus Vasa. Queen Elizabeth I was godmother at the child's christening on 30 September 1565, when the attendants included Helen and William Parr, the Marquess of Northampton. They married in 1571, but he died six months later. In 1574, Helen received substantial grants of land in Huntingdonshire from the Queen, (Pat. Rolls 17 Eliz). Helen

According to Noble,[43] Helena's second husband, Sir Thomas Gorges,[44] a Groom of the Chamber to Elizabeth I, presented John Shaxton to the living in 1599 in right of his wife. However, in the Episcopal Register, the presentation is listed 'pro hac vice' as Trinity College Cambridge.[45] Thomas and Helena are given as joint patrons when they presented Bartholomew Chamberlaine in 1600.[46]

married Thomas Gorges, and the Queen was godmother to their daughter Elizabeth. They were granted the treasure from a wrecked Spanish galleon in 1588 and built Longford Castle, south of Salisbury in Wiltshire. As Patron of Hemingford Abbots from 1574 to 1625, Helen was involved in the appointment of four rectors. See Charles Angell Bradford, *Helena, Marchioness of Northampton* (London: Allen & Unwin, 1936); also https://en.wikipedia.org/wiki/Helena_Snakenborg,_Marchioness_of_Northampton.

[43] William Mackreth Noble, 'Incumbents of the County of Huntingdon', *Transactions of the Cambridgeshire & Huntingdonshire Archaeological Society*, vol. iii, pt iv (1910), 'Hemingford Abbots', Noble, *Incumbents*, p. 120.

[44] https://en.wikipedia.org/wiki/Thomas_Gorges.

[45] LA, Register XXX (Episcopal Register); CCEd 324856. Cf. Kathleen Major, 'The Lincoln Diocesan Records', *Transactions of the Royal Historical Society*, 22 (1940), 39-66, doi:10.2307/3678581.

[46] CCEd 325001.

Figure 13 Sir Thomas Gorges

Figure 14 Helena, Marchioness of Northampton, 1603

In 1622, the patron was Christopher Brooke (c.1570–1628), who appointed his brother, Samuel Brooke, to the living. Christopher was originally from York, a barrister at Lincoln's Inn and an MP. He enjoyed minor renown as a poet. [47]

Charles I exercised the right of presentation in the case of Peter Heylyn in 1631.[48] When Theodore Crowley was appointed on 11 January 1632, the patron was Robert Paige of Leighton Bromswold, a barrister of Gray's Inn.[49] Robert Paige was Lord of the Manor of Hemingford Abbots.[50]

In Robert Paige's will of c. 1641, he gives instruction for the 'Royaltie and advousion of the parsonage of Hemingford' to be given to his brother John.[51] At the next presentation on 23 October 1632, when Simeon Paige, who was the son of John, was presented, the patrons are listed as Robertus Paige, Senior and Robertus Paige, Junior of Laighton,

---

[47] CCEd 188450. See https://doi.org/10.1093/ref:odnb/3538; https://www.historyofparliamentonline.org/volume/1604-1629/member/brooke-christopher-1570-1628; https://en.wikipedia.org/wiki/Christopher_Brooke. At Lincoln's Inn, he shared chambers and literary interests with John Donne.

[48] CCEd 228888.

[49] Paige is the usual spelling at this time. Page is found later.

[50] Robert Paige was christened in Hemingford Abbots in 1604. He also owned land in Hemingford Abbots, which he leased to Edmund Costeloe in 1630. Two years later, it was in the possession of Robert Currier and in 1646 was sold to Nathaniel Purkis and then in a further feoffment to T. Sheappard (Norris UMS/HEM A/08, 02, 04, 03).

[51] 'In the name of God Amen: I Robert Paige of Leighton in the County of Huntington Esquire being sicke of Bodie but of perfect memorie thanks bee given to God I doe committ my dust to the dust from whence itt came and my spiritt to him that gave it mee, my goods as followeth I doe give to my brother John Paige all the Royaltie and advousion of the parsonage of Hemingford and land bye emoluments in or about Hemingford Abbott's to be soul'd to pay my debts I doe give to either of my daughters five hundred pounds a piece to bee paid unto them when they shall Accomplish the age of eighteen years And I doe give to my said daughters twenty marks …', 'Will of Robert Paige or Page of Leighton, Huntingdonshire', 1642, The National Archives, Kew, PROB 11/188/65.

Huntingdonshire.[52] This was the last presentation by the Royalist Page family.[53]

Following the death of Robert Paige Jr., the Manor was divided into 'moieties' (halves). Robert Bernard, sergeant at law, and Mrs Newman then held the manorial rights.[54]

Figure 15 Bernard Arms

The next presentation, of Thomas Edmonds [Edmunds], was made in 1669, by which time the patronage had passed to Sir John Bernard [Barnard] (1630–79), 2nd Baronet, who sat in the Protectorate Parliaments as MP for Huntingdon from 1654 to 1660 and was unpopular as a landlord.[55] It is to be assumed that he also presented John Rowley in 1669, though no record is held.

In 1688, Sir Robert Bernard, 3rd baronet, MP for Huntingdonshire and High Sheriff of Cambridgeshire and Huntingdonshire,[56] presented Robert Hanbury. Following Bernard's death, in 1703, the advowson was

[52] For details of the complaints of parishioners against Robert Paige, Jr, see below, p. 42.

[53] Page, Proby and Ladds, pp. 304–09.

[54] Robert Bernard, MP, was created baronet in 1662. http://www.thepeerage.com/p13959.htm#i139583.

[55] http://www.historyofparliamentonline.org/volume/1660-1690/member/bernard-john-1630-79. This Lord of the Manor was a Parliamentarian from 1654 to 1660. See http://www.thepeerage.com/p13960.htm#i139592; https://en.wikipedia.org/wiki/Sir_John_Bernard,_2nd_Baronet.

[56] https://www.historyofparliamentonline.org/volume/1660-1690/member/bernard-sir-robert-1703. http://www.thepeerage.com/p13960.htm#i139598.

retained by his family, but the manor was sold. In 1712, when John Smith was presented, the patron is listed as Johannes [John] Bernard, curiously with the title of Bishop, together with Lady Anna Trevor, Mother and Guardian of John Bernard.[57] The John Bernard in question is Sir John Bernard, 4th baronet (c. 1695–1766), who was responsible for the next three presentations: Alexander Burrell (1714), Samuel Dickens (1714), and Charles Dickens (1748). Following John's death, two appointments were made by trustees[58] under the will of Sir Robert Bernard, 5th baronet (1740–89):[59] Thomas Stafford (1793) and Charles Greene (1797). On his death, the baronetcy became extinct; the advowson was inherited by Mary Bernard,[60] daughter of Sir John Bernard, 4th baronet, who married Robert Sparrow.[61] Their son, Brigadier-General Robert Bernard Sparrow (1773–1805), married Lady Olivia French Acheson (1778–1863) in 1797[62] and completed the building of Worlingham Hall, Suffolk, in 1800. He died at sea in 1805, aged 32, and was buried in Tobago. His widow re-built the 17th-century Bernard home, Brampton Park,[63] in 1820. Robert presented John Pery to the living in 1803.

[57] See CCEd 68972.

[58] Rogers Parker, Stanhope Pedley, John Smith.

[59] http://www.thepeerage.com/p13961.htm#i139607.

[60] http://www.thepeerage.com/p22235.htm#i222344.

[61] http://www.thepeerage.com/p3232.htm#i32318.

[62] http://www.thepeerage.com/p22235.htm#i222347.

[63] This house burnt down in 1907, and the later RAF base has been gradually replaced by housing since its closure in 2013.

Figure 16 Memorial to Robert Bernard Sparrow[64]

Robert married Lady Olivia French Acheson (1778–1863).[65] She was a pious and wealthy lady, who was noted for her philanthropy and devotion to the Church. She accumulated advowsons and founded national schools.[66] She presented clergy to the livings of Wyton, Grafham, Houghton, and Little Stukeley in addition to presenting Obins (1811) and Selwyn (1838) to Hemingford Abbots. She lived at Brampton Park until her death in 1863, having been a widow for fifty-eight years.

[64] In All Saints' Church, Worlingham.

[65] She was daughter of the first Earl of Gosford. http://www.thepeerage.com /p22235.htm#i222348. For her biography, see: https://st-neots.ccan.co.uk/content/catalogue_item/lady-olivia-sparrow-of-brampton-park-photograph-early-19th-century and https://www.hadleighhistory.org.uk/content/main-subjects /places/place/lady-olivia-sparrow-lady-of-the-manor.

[66] 'A National school was a school founded in 19th century England and Wales by the National Society for Promoting Religious Education. These schools provided elementary education, in accordance with the teaching of the Church of England, to the children of the poor.' https://en.wikipedia.org/wiki/National_school_(England_and_Wales).

LADY OLIVIA SPARROW,
From a picture by Richard Buckner, engraved by William Walker, 1854.

Figure 17 Lady Olivia Bernard Sparrow

The liberal nonconformist Bateman Brown is uncomplimentary about her in his *Reminiscences,* where he describes her as being 'a strong evangelical church woman of the most orthodox description … She was also, of course, a State and Church Tory of the old school'.[67] Her philanthropy

[67] Bateman Brown, *Reminiscences of Bateman Brown, J.P.,* a collection of articles first published in 1895–96 (Peterborough Advertiser Company, Peterborough, 1905) https://www.cantab.net/users/michael.behrend/repubs/brown_reminisc /pages/index.html [accessed 2 August 2020], pp. 42f. and passim. See also 'Potto Brown, Lady Olivia Sparrow, and William Loftie of Tandragee', Pottoingaround,

also comes in for some censure: 'Lady Sparrow was an illustration of the evils of lavish and indiscriminate giving. She by this means both pauperised and made hypocrites of the inhabitants of Brampton. It is stated that when some cottager saw her pass the window, she would get a Bible out and would be reading it when Lady Sparrow came to the door.'[68]

After Olivia's death in 1863, the patronage passed to the Duke of Manchester under her will, but it was not exercised. Selwyn died in September 1867, the advowson having been sold to Dennis Herbert earlier in the year.[69]

The sale of the 'common brewery'[70] in Huntingdon in 1864 had enabled the purchase of the advowson by Dennis Herbert specifically in order to present his half-brother, Henry Herbert, to the living on 25 October 1867.[71] The price paid for the advowson is not known, but a comparison might be nearby St Ives, where the advowson was offered for sale for £1,200 in 1866 (approx. £146,071 in 2020).[72] Advowsons were often auctioned. Their value depended both on the age and health of the clergyman in post at the time and the yield of the living. The value of the living in 1865 was £512 (£65,786 in 2020) plus house, whereas that of St Ives was £500, so the value of the advowson was comparable, although

2013. https://pottoingaround.wordpress.com/2013/07/06/potto-brown-lady-olivia-sparrow-and-william-loftie-of-tandragee/ [accessed 21 July 2021].

[68] Bateman Brown, p. 135.

[69] Dennis Herbert sold the family brewery in Huntingdon to James Marshall in 1864. It had been in the Herbert family since c. 1790. The brewery owned sixty-four public houses.

[70] 'Relatively large brewing concern, producing beer at a central brewery for distribution to a number of public houses, usually attached to the brewery by tie or direct ownership'. From *Glossary of Brewing Terminology* http://www.fatbadgers.co.uk/Britain/Glossary.htm.

[71] https://discovery.nationalarchives.gov.uk/details/r/0f075a7d-5a61-493e-bcca-1a9a00e3ac1b.

[72] Cf. David Yeandle, *A Victorian Curate: A Study of the Life and Career of the Rev. Dr John Hunt* (Cambridge, UK: Open Book Publishers, 2021), p. 72 https://doi.org/10.11647/OBP.0248.

the size of the parishes contrasted—518 lived in Hemingford Abbots and 3395 in St Ives.[73]

By the time of the next presentation, on 6 October 1911, of Francis Falkner Herbert, the patron was Caroline Herbert (d. 1917), sister of Henry Herbert.[74] Members of the Herbert family were responsible for presenting to the Bishop eleven rectors from 1867 to 1977. The Monarch appoints the successor when an incumbent becomes a bishop, as in 1977. For the next six rectors, the patrons were representatives of the late Henry Herbert: Frith (1925); George (1926); Ayre (1931); Clements (1932); Balleine (1936), and Denison (1946). For the appointment of Stevens, Bawtree, and Young, Dennis, 2nd Lord Hemingford was patron, although he was persuaded by the Diocese to take the Archdeacon of Huntingdon, David Young, who became Bishop of Ripon, after which the next presentation devolved to the Crown, and Richard Sledge was appointed.

Until 1978, part of the endowment of the benefice consisted of agricultural glebe land, which was owned by the incumbent by right of his office. Income from letting it formed part of his stipend. Under the Endowments and Glebe Measure of 1976 this was transferred to the Diocesan Board of Finance, which took over its management. Diocesan income from former glebe lands contributes towards the pay of parochial clergy.

In 1986, Parliament approved the Patronage (Benefices) Measure, which updated the 1896 Benefices Act and others dating back to 1588. The registration of patrons under this measure included that of Nicholas, 3rd Lord Hemingford, in 1988.

David Young (1977) and subsequently Richard Sledge, as Archdeacons of Huntingdon, were also appointed as part-time Rectors of Hemingford Abbots and lived in the Rectory. The Rectory at Hemingford Abbots would continue to be linked to the Benefice while it was the

---

[73] See the entries for Selwyn and Fosbroke in *Crockford's Clerical Directory* for 1865 (London: Horace Cox, 1865).

[74] The mandate for the induction incorrectly states that he was Rector, rather than Vicar, of Hemingford Grey: https://discovery.nationalarchives.gov.uk/details/r/3be4d1d3-2e2d-4246-b5dc-6713390877bd.

archdeacon's residence.[75] In 1988, the Bishop of Ely relieved archdeacons of their parochial responsibilities. He also decided that the patronages of both Hemingfords would be suspended for five years; that the two parishes would be served by the same priest-in-charge for an experimental period, initially of five years; that Stephen Talbot would be appointed; and that he would live in the larger parish of Hemingford Grey.

During this activity in 1988, the patrons and churchwardens of the two parishes had several meetings and much correspondence with the Bishop and Archdeacon of Huntingdon and diocesan officers. Concern was expressed that parish rights, including the rectory house, should be protected rather than being vested in the Diocesan Board of Finance, and assurances were given that all the parties would be consulted. This was reassuring, but nevertheless concerns continued to be expressed in the national press that diocesan officers advising bishops would increasingly override the wishes of parishioners and patrons.

Since 1988, the suspension of the patronage of Hemingford Abbots has been renewed every five years while it has been linked with Hemingford Grey or Houghton and Wyton, and the deanery boundaries have been changed (2004).[76] Hemingford Abbots has been served by three priests-in-charge during these thirty-three years, with several other clergy and Licensed Lay Ministers supporting the parish during the interregna.

[75] Correspondence from Bishop of Ely to Churchwardens of Hemingford Abbots, 5 May 1989: 'So long as the parish remains in suspension the Rectory will remain benefice property.'

[76] The Church of England website on Pastoral Organisation states: 'Following consultation, the right of presentation to a benefice can be suspended by the Bishop for a period lasting no longer than five years. It is possible to renew the suspension, but again for no longer than five years.' https://www.elydiocese.org/parish-support/pastoral-organization/vacancies-and-suspension-of-presentation.php.

Church Building, Burial Ground, Archives

The first church at Hemingford Abbots was probably a wooden struc-
ture. This was replaced by the first stone building around 1190 on the
site of the later chancel.[77] The present font dates from this time. Wooden
buildings were more vulnerable to fires, such as devastated Peterborough in 1116 and Lincoln in 1141. Stone towers and spires were suscep-
tible to collapse, as shown by the earthquake and storm damage in 1185
and 1548 at Lincoln, at Ely in 1323, and both Hemingford Grey and All
Saints', St Ives in a storm in 1741.[78]

It is likely that the dedication to St Margaret of Antioch dates from
the time of the first stone church, since dedications to Margaret became
popular in the thirteenth century. Margaret was fabled as a slayer of
dragons and was also the patron saint of childbearing.[79] There are approximately eighty dedications to her in this period. A wooden plaque
was inscribed by David Peace at about the time of the Millennium cele-
brations, which includes details of her life around the edge.[80] Her biography is generally held to be fictitious.

[77] Cf. 'Conjectured Medieval Settlement Pattern of the Hemingfords',
https://www.huntingdonshire.gov.uk/media/2326/hemingfords-ca-character-
assessment-adopted-june-2008.pdf, p. 7.

[78] Bernard E. Dorman, *The Story of Ely and its Cathedral* (Norwich: B.E. Dorman,
1968); J. H. Srawley, *The Story of Lincoln Minster* (London, R. Tuck); J. L. Cartwright, *The Pictorial History of Peterborough Cathedral: Cathedral Church of St. Peter,
St. Paul and St. Andrew* (London: Pitkin Pictorials, 1966); 'Hemingford Grey.' An
Inventory of the Historical Monuments in Huntingdonshire. London: His Majesty's Stationery Office, 1926. 133–36. British History Online. Web. 3 November
2021. http://www.british-history.ac.uk/rchme/hunts/pp133-136.

[79] https://downhamchurch.org.uk/history.html. In detail, see https://en.wikipe-
dia.org/wiki/Margaret_the_Virgin.

[80] 'July 20th St Margaret Virgin and Martyr, A.D 278 daughter of Theodosius a
Pagan priest of Antioch, but became a Christian. Olybrius Roman Governor of
the district wished to marry her but was rejected. She was thrown into a dungeon
and tortured. She refused to deny her faith and was beheaded. Crowned as a
Martyr. Her emblems are a palm and dragon.'

Figure 18 St Margaret plaque, inscribed by David Peace

A hymn was written for the feast of St Margaret, which is on 20 July, and has been sung on her name day to the tune Llanfair (with Alleluias) in St Margaret's church.

> 1. Pious Margaret, Virgin blessed,
> Witness for your faith oppressed,
> Though assailed by trials and pain,
> Christ you served for endless gain.

> 2. Spurning him who bade you wed,
> Till for Christ your blood was shed,
> Antioch's lord you did decline,
> With your martyr's crown to shine.

3. Satan once in dragon's guise,
Swallowed you, his longed-for prize,
But you, as a child new-born,
Sprang forth from that beast forlorn.

4. Holy Margaret, tend your church,
Shepherd us in heavenward search,
That your flock, all perils past,
Pastures pure may find at last.

David Yeandle

The basis of the present church at Hemingford Abbots dates from the late twelfth century. It was located where the present chancel stands. There was a rood screen west of the chancel, with access up a staircase set into the twelfth-century pier on the north side. Remains of the rood-light pulley fixture are evident in the eastern tie-beam of the nave.[81]

Later, the nave was extended westwards, and a Lady Chapel was added on the south side. A north aisle, dedicated to Nicholas, the patron saint of travellers, was added in the thirteenth century, and the Lady Chapel was incorporated into a south aisle. Buttresses in each aisle supported the tower. Under the buttress in the south aisle, there is a carved royal head, and outside, two mass dials are inscribed into the thirteenth-century stonework.

---

[81] Although Henry VIII's injunctions of 1538 prohibited all candles and tapers burning before images, it expressly exempted 'the light that commonly goeth across the church by the rood-loft', and these were allowed to continue for a while. However, the destruction of roods was soon legalised by Thomas Cromwell and much desecration followed. See '1538 Second Injunctions', *Henry VIII, the Reign* https://www.henryviiithereign.co.uk/1538-second-injunctions.html.

Figure 19 Entrance to rood loft

Figure 20 Mass dials on the south wall[82]

[82] The shadow of the central gnomon in the mass dial would have indicated 9:00 am on one of the radial lines, marking the hour when the bell would be rung for

In the fourteenth century, the central tower was replaced with a substantial new tower. This was set into the west end of the nave, probably to be further from a narrow canal for boats that carried building materials and other goods from the river to the high street. The spire was added, and the nave roof raised in the fifteenth century. The twenty-two angels were carved in the early 1500s.[83]

Some generations were more active than others over the subsequent four centuries. Repairs to the spire were needed from time to time, including 1822, 1863, 1887, 1932, and 1950. Significant works were carried out in the early 1900s, including the rebuilding of the chancel and the installation of the chancel's east window in memory of the Rev. Henry Herbert.

Mass on Sundays and feast days. The two dials would have been used in different seasons of the year. The shadow at noon on Midsummer's Day would have fallen on the noon-line of one of the dials. Although such sundials became obsolete after the Reformation and the installation of the striking church clock, they provided helpful indications of the passage of the hours between sunrise and sunset. See Stephen Friar, *A Companion to the English Parish Church* (Godalming, Surrey: Bramley Books, 1998), pp. 436–7.

[83] See Charles Beresford, *Angel Roof Carvings at St Margaret's Church, Hemingford Abbots* (2017).

Figure 21 The chancel in 2019

The consecrated land adjacent to the church has been used for inter-
ments for many centuries.[84] The earliest stone memorials have survived
since the eighteenth century. Written archives, including registers of
baptisms, marriages, and burials, have survived from the early seventeenth century. The Archdeaconry index of wills began in 1479.

---

[84] Cf. the will of Thomas Newman in 1490: 'burial in the cemetery of the church
of the blessed virgin Margaret of hemyngford Abb.'

Churchwardens, Representation, Benefactors

A proportion of each generation of the laity living in the parish has valued the continuation of an active church with a dedicated priest and a well-maintained building and churchyard. This has involved volunteer parishioners taking turns to carry out a variety of responsibilities and functions. They were led previously by the parish clerk and now by two or three churchwardens, who are elected annually by the residents of the parish.

A wider group of people is elected at regular intervals to form a committee, previously called the vestry and now the parochial church council, to represent the parishioners on the electoral roll—those who are members of the church. The council is normally chaired by the priest-in-charge, and it oversees in general the ways in which the church functions.

The finances of such a local voluntary organization are linked with the Ely diocesan organization. Income from the rental of church lands and buildings, together with a share of the income from the parish, contributes towards clergy stipends and other costs, such as church schools and the cathedral. Nationally, glebe land ceased to belong to individual incumbents and passed to diocesan boards of finance under the 1976 Endowments and Glebe Measure. The minimum level of clergy stipends is recommended each year by the Central Stipends Authority.

The parish covers the costs of resourcing worship, the church buildings and their contents, and maintaining the churchyard for all residents of the parish. Income from the regular worshippers to maintain and improve the church is augmented by the Friends of St Margaret's, a charity that is registered with the Charities Commission and organizes a biennial flower festival.

There have been several major benefactions to the church over the years that have also made possible significant improvements to the building. Income from such benefactions and that raised by the flower festivals has made it viable for the small number of families in the village and worshippers from elsewhere to meet the costs of maintaining regular worship.

Clergy Roles

The needs, concerns, and wishes of clergy and laity have changed radically over the centuries. Some issues have changed, as society has become increasingly secular and multi-faith. Questions arise in each generation, such as: Does the incumbent's role cover every resident of the parish or only those who are sympathetic to the current policies of the Church of England? How best can the incumbent interpret the commitment made on induction to 'care for the souls of the parish' across a range of Christian churchmanship, from Anglo-Catholic to Evangelical? How can people be helped to feel welcome at Eucharistic services if they have not been baptized or confirmed? How can clergy become familiar to residents in several small parishes and help them to flourish? How can the elderly and infirm feel valued, those in midlife feel involved, and youngsters be helped to understand Christian values? Such questions have faced each generation in various ways, and inevitably, clergy have coped with varying degrees of success.

This book is intended to provide a glimpse into some of their lives, but it is dependent on a few archives and memories, so cannot do justice to their remarkable efforts and many achievements. There is also little documentation about the significance of the spouses of the incumbents and the lay ministers, in supporting them through the challenges that most have faced by the nature of their calling.

Clergy before the Reformation

The Ramsey *Cartulary*[85] mentions that during the time of Hugh, who was Bishop of Lincoln from 1186 to 1200, the Abbot of Ramsey, Robert, made a gift of the church of St Margaret, Hemingford Abbots, to the Prior and monks of St Ives. This was 'in perpetual possession, saving the perpetual vicarage of Master Aristotle and his successors who pay annually to the church of St Ives …'[86] However, as mentioned above (p. 16), the priory reverted to the abbey in 1209, following its destruction by fire, until it passed to John Wyseman at the Reformation.

The patronage of Hemingford Grey was held by Huntingdon Priory until its dissolution.[87]

Some of the registers of the Bishops of Lincoln have been published by the Lincoln Record Society, showing, for example, that John Clarel was presented by the Abbots of Ramsey to Hemingford Abbots in 1252–53 and that no further appointments were made here until Clarel's death in 1295.[88]

The thirteenth century saw a decline in the income of Ramsey Abbey, and a gradual shift in its source from grain crops to sheep farming. Abbot William de Godmanchester mortgaged resources to buy more productive land, including some at Hemingford Abbots. His successor, John

---

[85] Cf. 'Ramsey Abbey, Cambridgeshire, was founded in 969 and rapidly became one of the richest and most important Benedictine houses in the country. It was famous for its school and library, and a thriving market town grew up around it, despite its isolated position in the Fens. The cartulary contains a range of legal, financial and ecclesiastical documents dating from 974 to 1436, although the greater part was compiled in the fourteenth century. It is particularly important for the study of manorial and economic history …' Frontmatter (2012), in: W. Hart and P. Lyons, eds., *Cartularium Monasterii de Rameseia* (Cambridge Library Collection–Rolls; Cambridge: Cambridge University Press), pp. i-ii.

[86] Hart and Lyons, vol. II, p. 177. See also Page, Proby and Ladds, pp. 304–09.

[87] See Noble, *Incumbents*, pp. 119f. For details of pre-Reformation clergy, see the table, Appendix, pp. 171f.

[88] It seems likely that the name was John rather than Robert Clarel. Ladds, writing to Robert Balleine (25 October 1937), criticises Wise and Noble for being careless and inconsistent in different papers.

de Sawtrey (1286–1318), liquidated £50 of a £240 debt owed to Sir William de Bereford.[89] However, the building of the westward extension of St Margaret's had continued during this time, and the next appointment in 1295 was Robert de Sautre, who may have been related to the Abbot.

Raftis notes that 'By 1300 he was forced to establish a sinking fund by which his heavy debts could be wiped out.'[90] In 1310, the Prior and monks objected and declared that they would refuse to sing the services in the Abbey unless they were relieved of all liability for the debts. On 19 June, the abbots made an assignment of the revenues of Hemingford Abbots and Ellington to discharge them.[91]

The population of England more than doubled in the two and a half centuries between the Domesday Survey of 1086, when it numbered between 1.75 and 2.25 million, and the Black Death of 1348, when it was between 4.5 and 6 million.[92] It has been estimated that between 40% and 60% of the national population died in 1348–49 and a further 20% in the outbreak of 1361–62.

---

[89] Sir William de Bereford (d. 1326) was an eminent judge with land in eight counties. (ODNB) His branch of the Beresford family ended with the death of his grandson Sir Baldwin in 1401. Douglas K. Beresford and Brian K. Beresford, *The House of Beresford*, vol. 1, 1227–1727 (Beresford Family Society, 2011), p. 176. £240 in 1300 would equate to about £275,000 in 2021. It is not known whether the debt was fully repaid.

[90] J. A. Raftis, *The Estates of Ramsey Abbey: A Study in Economic Growth and Organization*, Studies and Texts Pontifical Institute of Mediaeval Studies, 3 (Toronto: PIMS, 1957), p. 237. See 'Epistolae Abbatis Joh. de Sautre' (no. 59), in W.D. Macray, ed., *Chronicon Abbatiae Rameseiensis: A Saec. x. Usque Ad an. Circiter 1200: In Quatuor Partibus. Partes I., II., III., Iterum Post Th. Gale, Ex Chartulario in Archivis Regni Servato, Pars IV. Nunc Primum Ex Aliis Codicubus*, Rerum Britannicarum Medii Aevi Scriptores, or, Chronicles and Memorials of Great Britain and Ireland during the Middle Ages (Longman, 1886) https://books.google.co.uk/books?id=-KgUAAAAQAAJ, Appendix, p. 394.

[91] *Ibid.* Cf. Robert Balleine, 'In Olden Days', *Hemingford Abbots Parish Magazine*, c. 1937.

[92] J. Hatcher, John, *Plague, Population and the English Economy 1348–1530*, 2nd ed. (London: Palgrave, 1977), quoted in: Michael Wickes, *A History of Huntingdonshire* (Chichester: Phillimore, 1995), p. 62.

The population of Huntingdonshire of those aged 14 and over in 1348 was between 25,000 and 35,000. This declined to 14,169 by 1377 and then to 11,299 aged 15 and over in 1381.[93] This figure is comparable to the population in 1086, when the Domesday Book stated that there were 2,914 heads of household in the county. Taking serfs and others not recorded this would give a rough population of 10,000–15,000 people.[94]

Little is known about the clergy in the two centuries before the Reformation other than Michael Ravendale, Lawrence Booth, and Robert Bellamy.

Ravendale was a clerk in Chancery when instituted to Hemingford Abbots in 1361.[95] Booth was born in Barton, Lancashire in 1420 and studied civil and canon law at Pembroke Hall, Cambridge. He later became Master and then Chancellor of the University. During this time, he held several livings in plurality, including Hemingford Abbots from 1444 to 1448. This was a common practice at the time, the actual work in the parish being carried out by a priest who received a small proportion of the income of the living as a stipend. In 1456, Booth was appointed Dean of St Paul's and entered politics as Lord Keeper of the Privy Seal. In the following year, he was tutor and guardian of Edward, Prince of Wales, son of Henry VI. He was nominated Bishop of Durham by the Pope and consecrated in 1457 by his half-brother, William Booth, who was Archbishop of York from 1452 to 1464. Lawrence Booth supported the Lancastrian cause in the Wars of the Roses and was under a cloud when Edward IV ascended the throne in 1461, but he had accepted the new order by 1464 and did not support the 1471 uprising. He was appointed Lord Chancellor in 1473 but retired after a year and was Archbishop of York from 1476 until his death in 1480. Bellamy (1476) became a prebendary of Lincoln in 1483.[96]

---

[93] Lord Treasurer's Remembrancer's Enrolled Accounts, quoted in: Charles Oman, *The Great Revolt of 1381* (London: Greenhill, 1989), Appendix II, pp. 162ff.; R. Trevor Davies, *Documents Illustrating the History of Civilization in Medieval England (1066–1500)* (New York: Barnes & Noble, 1969), p. 274.

[94] Wickes, *ibid.*

[95] Cf. Weale, n. 13, p. 362. On the office, see https://en.wikipedia.org/wiki/Clerk_of_the_Crown_in_Chancery.

[96] Browne Willis, *A Survey of the Cathedrals of York ...* (T. Osborne in Gray's Inn and T. Bacon in Dublin, 1742), p. 165.

Clergy and Patrons since the Reformation

Reign of Henry VIII (1509–47)

John London, Rector (1524–44)

Patron: The Abbot and Monks of Ramsey

John London[97] was a commissioner for dissolution. He was a Fellow of New College Oxford from 1505 and became a Doctor of Civil Law in 1519 at the age of 33. In the same year, he became a prebendary of York and soon afterwards was Domestic Chaplain to Archbishop Warham.

In 1522, London was appointed a prebendary of Lincoln and treasurer of the cathedral. So, in 1524, when Lewes Williams died, while incumbent of Hemingford Abbots in the Lincoln diocese, John London would have been in a strong position to influence the Abbot and monks of Ramsey Abbey as patrons of the parish.[98] He added Hemingford Abbots to the livings that he already held in plurality: Ewelme, Oxfordshire, from 1502; Stockbury, Kent, since before 1511; and Adderbury, Oxfordshire.

In 1526, he returned to New College Oxford as Master, and was Dean of Osney (Oxford) and Wallingford (13 miles south of Oxford). As no other Rector was appointed to Hemingford Abbots until Percival Lego, after John London's death, it is likely that he retained the income and that curates such as John Mane were employed.

From 1535, he was one of Thomas Cromwell's most active commissioners for the visitations of religious houses.[99] The gathering of information

---

[97] CCEd Person ID: 84433. The details from the CCEd are not recorded in the text and footnotes for subsequent clergy. These details can be found by consulting the tables in the Appendix, on pp. 172ff.

[98] In the context of London's appointment, Weale (p. 69) notes, 'Hemingford Abbots appears to have been blessed with scholars, although how many were resident in their parish it is difficult to assess.'

[99] G. Hodgett, *Tudor Lincolnshire* (Lincoln, 1975), p. 9 writes: 'In 1539, Dr London led a Commission in Lincolnshire, assisted by gentry like Sir John Heneage, which acted to suppress ten houses, including Thornton Abbey, with Crowland

was followed by the surrender of the priories and monasteries, which were then stripped of everything that had a pecuniary value. Relics that could not be removed were defaced and destroyed during 1536–39. It is likely that ornaments and vestments were removed from John London's parish of Hemingford Abbots, with images desecrated, wall paintings and the doom painting over the east wall around the chancel arch white-washed. The restored, beautifully decorated ceilure at the east end of the nave retains inscriptions on the beams.[100]

Figure 22 Ceilure at the east end of the nave

probably the last one, in December 1539.' Dr London wrote to Cromwell in July 1539 that he had finished his work in many minor local houses and also at Beau-vale and Newstead. Adrian Gray, *Restless Souls: Pilgrim Roots: The Turbulent History of Christianity in Nottinghamshire and Lincolnshire* (Retford: Bookworm, 2020). [100] On the easternmost tie-beam, above where the doom would have been, can be read, 'Venite benedicti patris mei et [ite] maledicti in ignem eternum' ('Come ye blessed of my father, and depart ye cursed into eternal fire', Matthew 25:34 & 41). The westernmost beam has the inscription 'Pray for Wyllm basele and for hys wyvs.' See Charles Beresford, *Angel Roof Carvings*, p. 9; Aymer Vallance, *English Church Screens* (Batsford, 1936), p. 14; 'Hemingford Abbots | British History Online' https://www.british-history.ac.uk/rchme/hunts/pp130-133, p. 132.

When the commissioner Thomas Bedyll[101] visited Ramsey Abbey, in 1535, he found that the Abbot and monks were content with royal supremacy.[102] The wealth of the abbey had been enhanced by many benefactions over the centuries[103] and by dues from Hemingford Abbots and other parishes.[104] However, the abbey did not escape being dissolved two years later.[105] During the twelfth and thirteenth centuries, there had been approximately eighty monks in residence at Ramsey Abbey, but by 1534 this had shrunk to thirty-four, including Thoms Ffyld from Hemingford, one of the youngest or junior monks at the Dissolution. He was granted a life pension of V li (£5) per annum.[106]

Bedyll and John London were fellows of New College, Oxford, and Bedyll was one of Henry VIII's chaplains. London sought Bedyll's support when Cromwell withdrew his favour from London, following increasing reports of him 'using the opportunities as Visitor to solicit nuns and others.' Bedyll died in 1537 and Cromwell in 1540. London died in prison in February 1543/4,[107] having been accused of perjury in attacking

---

[101] ODNB, https://doi.org/10.1093/ref:odnb/1943.

[102] The Abbey held 25 hides in the two Hemingfords, more than any other parish in Huntingdonshire or its neighbouring counties, of a total of 387 hides in 8 counties. Wise and Noble, p. 60.

[103] E.g., Deed XXVII is an agreement made between 1267 and 1286. Emma, the widow of Berengarius le Moyne granted her estates to the Abbey and Monastery of Ramsey, 'reserving only till her death, lands and tenements in Hemingford which the Abbot had granted her as dowry.' Wise and Noble, p. 82.

[104] Charter XVI confirms the right of Ramsey Abbey to demand 40 shillings from the church of Hemingford and a portion of the tithes from the demesne lands. The seal states that this was granted on 5 March 1343 by John, Bishop of Norwich. Wise and Noble, p. 79.

[105] Ramsey Abbey and its land were sold to Sir Richard Williams, alias Cromwell, in 1540. Much of the stone was used for the gatehouse at Hinchingbrooke House, Godmanchester Church, Gonville and Caius College, King's College, and Trinity College in Cambridge.

[106] Wise and Noble, p. 147.

[107] He died in February 1544, but before the change in the calendar from the Julian to the Gregorian calendar this would have been recorded as 1543. The legal new year moved from 25 March to 1 January in 1752.

Archbishop Cranmer.[108] His chequered career also included doing public penance for adultery with a mother and daughter in Oxford.[109]

The dissolution of the monasteries and the subsequent sale of monastic lands by the crown caused a radical change in land ownership in Huntingdonshire. About a third of the land area of the county passed to the crown. Twenty-seven of the thirty-three parishes that had belonged to monasteries had been granted or sold by 1600, either to individuals or to the deans and chapters of churches, notably Peterborough and Westminster.

John Mane, Curate (1540)

This is probably John Man [variant Mane], from Writtle in Essex. He obtained his BA in 1533 and MA in 1537 from New College, Oxford, where he was a fellow. He proceeded BCL in 1540. He was rector of Great Horwood, 1551, of Broughton, 1552, and of Adstock (Bucks.). He died in 1565.[110]

---

[108] Weale (p. 69) notes, 'How much time he was to give to his cure of souls it is difficult to say, as he was a canon of York and prebendary of Bilton until 1542. In 1522 he became treasurer of Lincoln. He held the vicarage of Atterbury (Oxford) until 1542. (373) In Foxe's Acts and Monuments he is described as "heartless in his dealings with Lutheran suspects at Oxford (374) in 1528 and at Windsor in 1543". He was totally opposed to Cranmer, and would probably have been an ally of the conservative bishop John Longland.'

[109] 'This Dr. London, for his incontinency, afterwards did open penance in Oxford, having two smocks on his shoulders for Mrs. Thykked and Mrs. Jennyngs, the mother and the daughter: with one of whom he was taken by Henry Plankney in his gallery, being his sister's son. This was known to a number in Oxford and elsewhere, many years after living, as well as to Loud, the relater of it in a letter to Mr. Fox.' https://en.wikipedia.org/wiki/John_London_(priest).

[110] *Alumni Oxonienses: The Members of the University of Oxford, 1500–1714: Their Parentage Birthplace, and Year of Birth, with a Record of Their Degrees / (Oxford, 1891),* p. 964. http://hdl.handle.net/2027/pst.000007713354.

Reign of Edward VI (1547–53)

Adrian Gray notes the turbulence between 1547 and 1558: 'in a few short years, England varied from the strongly evangelical short reign of Edward VI to the repressive restoration of Catholicism under Mary, and eventually back to something of the middle ground under Elizabeth.'[111]

Percival Lego, Rector (1544–55)[112]

Patron: John Wyseman (*pro hac vice*)[113]

Percival Lego was appointed on 6 February 1544. In the Lincoln Episcopal Register he is listed as 'clerk' but in the *Liber Cleri* for his Aspenden appointment as 'dom[inus]' i.e. he held a bachelor's degree, though the university is not known.[114] He was Vicar of Aspenden, Herts, at his death in 1555.[115] An anonymous death is reported for the parish on 29 March 1555.[116] This probably refers to Lego.[117]

---

[111] Gray, p. 113.

[112] Variants: Percivallus and Parcivallus Lego. Will proved 1556.

[113] See https://www.historyofparliamentonline.org/volume/1509-1558/member/wiseman-john-1515–58.

[114] CCEd 39968.

[115] Cf. *UK, Extracted Probate Records, 1269-1975:* 'Name: Lego, Percival; Dates: 1556; Place: Aspenden, Lincolnshire, England; Book: Calendar of Wills Proved and of Administrations Granted in the Commissary Court of the Peculiar and Exempt Jurisdiction of Groby, 1580–1800. Collection: Lincolnshire and Huntingdonshire: - Calendar of Lincolnshire Wills, 1601–52, Calendars of Huntingdonshire Wills, 1479-1652; Volume: Calendar of Wills and Administrations in the Archdeaconry of Huntingdon Now Preserved in the Probate Registry of Peterborough. Chapter: Transcripts of Wills in Volumes 1–12, 12a–19. Text: 1556 Lego, Percival, parson of Aspenden 10 125.' From Ancestry.com.

[116] Calendar of Patent Rolls 1554–1555 (Presentations, etc.) CCEd 170635

[117] Cf. Noble, p. 120, fn. 1 'Will proved 1556'. CCEd 121521.

Reign of Mary I (1553–58)

Thomas Thompson, Rector (1555)

Patron: The Crown (Queen Mary)

Thompson was presented to Hemingford Abbots on 29 March 1555.[118] His tenure was a little over a year. 'The former Meaux monk is known to have died in the archdeaconry of Stowe on 18 April 1563, so he could have been the Thomas Thompson, clerk, presented by the crown to the rectory of Hemingford Abbots in the diocese of Lincoln in 1555.'[119] He was a prebendary of Lincoln in 1553.[120]

Arthur Yeldard, Rector (1556–99)[121]

Patron: The Crown (Queen Mary)

Yeldard was presented on 24 August 1556, during the reign of Queen Mary. He survived the transition to Protestantism under Elizabeth I. The forms of the name Arthur Heldarde, Arthur Yelderd, and Arthur Yeldard are recorded with reference to Hemingford Abbots. He was born, c. 1526. He held the Cambridge degrees of MA, BD, and DD. He enjoyed the support of influential patrons and had an illustrious career, becoming *inter alia* President of Trinity College, Oxford from 1559 to 1599 and Vice-Chancellor of Oxford University in 1580.[122] Yeldard issued 'Letters Denunciatory of Excommunication' in the final year of his forty-three-year incumbency, during which he employed a succession of curates. He died in 1599.

---

[118] CCEd 170635.

[119] *Yorkshire Archaeological Society*, Record Series, 150 (1995), p. 164.

[120] England & Wales, *Calendar of the Principal Ecclesiastical Dignitaries*, 314–1853; Name: Thomas Thomson; Diocese: Lincoln; Event Date: 17 Dec 1553. From Ancestry.com.

[121] His name is recorded as *Yeldare* by Noble, p. 120, apparently a misspelling. See CCEd 7492.

[122] For full details, see ODNB https://doi.org/10.1093/ref:odnb/30210; https://en.wikipedia.org/wiki/Arthur_Yeldard; https://venn.lib.cam.ac.uk/.

Reign of Elizabeth I (1558–1603)

Anthony Ford, Curate (1572)

Ford was curate in 1572. He became Vicar of Croft in 1573 and died in 1576.

Nicholas Yeldon, Curate (1573)

Nicholas Yeldon is probably the same as Nicholas Yeldard, Perpetual Vicar of Fenstanton (resigned 1597). He may have been the brother of Arthur Yeldard, who was Rector at the time.[123]

Henry Mariat, Curate (1574–78)

Henry Mariat (1572–97), variously spelled Mariat and Marret with reference to Hemingford Abbots, is recorded as curate in 1574 and 1578. Marriatte and Mariott are variant spellings. He became Vicar of Doddington, to the west of Lincoln, in 1577.

Christopher Lewis, Curate (1585)

Christopher Lewis is recorded as curate in 1585, ordained deacon and priest on 5 February 1577. This would appear to be the man who became vicar of Great Stukeley, Huntingdonshire, 1585–87 and later rector of Saltfleet by St Peter, Lincolnshire, 1587–89.

Humphrey Price, Curate (1591)

There is little evidence for Humphrey Price save for an entry in the Clerical Subsidy records as curate.[124]

---

[123] Thomas Warton, *The Life of Sir Thomas Pope, Founder of Trinity College, Oxford* (T. Davies, T. Becket, T. Walters, and J. Fletcher, 1772), p. 370.

[124] CCEd 230226.

George Cooke, Curate (1597–99)

Cooke is recorded as curate in 1597 and 1599. His ordination was in 1583; he was curate in Hollywell in 1585, 1587, and 1588.[125]

John Shaxton, Rector (1598–1600)

Patron: Trinity College, Cambridge (*pro hac vice*)

Shaxton was appointed by his old college on 8 February 1598. He held the degrees of BA 1587/8; MA 1591; BD 1598. Elected a fellow of Trinity in 1589, he was Deputy Proctor in 1591.[126] He died in post after only one year in early 1600.

Bartholomew Chamberlen, Rector (1600–21)

Patron: Thomas Gorges, Knight, and Dame Helen, Marchioness of Northampton, his wife

Bartholomew Chamberlen [variant Chamberlaine][127] was appointed rector of Hemingford Abbots on 20 February 1600.[128] The Parish registers of Baptisms, Marriages and Burials begin in 1604.[129] A variant spelling of the name is Chamberlen. He is distinct from Bartholomew Chamberlaine, Vicar of Great Stukeley, who died in 1608.[130] He was born at Shipton-under-Wychwood, Oxfordshire, in 1545.[131] He held the Oxford degrees of BA 1566; MA 1570; BD 1576; and DD 1578/9. He was a scholar (7 June 1563, aged 17) and fellow of Trinity College, Oxford, fellow of Trinity College, Cambridge, 1567. He was ordained priest in 1576 by the Bishop of Rochester. He evidently held several parishes in plurality. He

---

[125] CCEd 142521.

[126] See https://venn.lib.cam.ac.uk/.

[127] See https://venn.lib.cam.ac.uk/.

[128] CCEd.

[129] Parish Registers and Bishop's Transcripts at Huntingdon Record Office AH28/40/1–4.

[130] CCEd.

[131] 'Parish Register Name: Bartholomew Chamberlaine; Event Type: Baptism; Baptism Date: 16 Jan 1545.' From Ancestry.com.

was appointed rector of Abbots Morton in 1578; perpetual vicar of Burford in 1578 (resigned 1586); rector of Holywell cum Needingworth in 1579 (resigned 1601). He proceeded DD (Cantab.) by incorporation in 1585. He is recorded as rector of Sandy in 1597, which he resigned in 1600. In addition to being rector of Hemingford Abbots, he was vicar of Hemingford Grey from 1602 to 1606. He was the only priest in the seventeenth century to hold both incumbencies.[132] He is recorded still as rector of Hemingford Abbots in 1614[133] and probably died in post in 1621. He was the author of: *A Sermon Preached at Farington in Barkeshire, the Seuenteene of Februarie, 1587 At the Buriall of the Right Honorable the Ladie Anne Countes of Warwicke, Daughter to the Duke of Sommerset His Grace, and Widowe of the Right Worshipfull Sir Edward Vmpton Knight. By Bartholomew Chamberlaine, Doctor of Diuinitie.*, 1591 and *The Passion of Christ and the benefits thereby by Bartholomew Chamberlaine, Doctor in Diuinitie* (1595/1612). He had a son, William (1601).[134]

Reign of James I (1603–25)

Samuel Brooke, Rector (1622–31)[135]

Patron: Christopher Brooke[136]

Samuel Brooke (1574–1632), was the third son of Robert Brooke (c. 1531–99), a merchant and lord mayor of York, and his wife, Jane (d. 1604), the daughter of Christopher Maltby of Thornton in Pickering Lythe.[137] He was educated at Westminster School and Trinity College, Cambridge (pensioner c. 1592; scholar 1593; BA 1595; MA 1598).

---

[132] See Noble, pp. 119–21, Incumbents of St Margaret's, Hemingford Abbots and St James's, Hemingford Grey.

[133] CCEd.

[134] *Alumni Oxonienses,*1500–1714, p. 257.

[135] See CCEd; https://venn.lib.cam.ac.uk/; *Alumni Oxonienses, 1500–1714*, p. 189.

[136] See above, p. 21.

[137] For full biographical details, see ODNB https://doi.org/10.1093/ref:odnb/3555 and https://en.wikipedia.org/wiki/Samuel_Brooke.

He was appointed rector of Hemingford Abbots by his brother Christopher on 6 March 1622.[138] On 23 December 1599, he was ordained deacon and priest at Peterborough. From 1600 to 1615, he was chaplain of Trinity. In December 1601, he officiated at the marriage of John Donne, who was a friend of his brother Christopher. Samuel proceeded BD in 1607 and became a chaplain to Henry, Prince of Wales in about 1610. Christopher became known as a poet and Samuel as a dramatist, writing Latin plays. In 1612, he was appointed professor of divinity at Gresham's College, London, later becoming chaplain to the King. Afterwards, he concentrated on theological work. In 1615, he proceeded DD (incorporated at Oxford in 1621), and in June 1616, 'he delivered a dissertation, *De auxilio divinae gratiae*, in which he attacked Calvin and, while claiming not to be his disciple, supported the Dutch theologian Arminius in his rebuttal of the doctrine of predestination'.[139]

During his full career, he was also Master of Trinity College, Cambridge, 1629–31; Rector of St Margaret, Lothbury, London, 1618–27; Rector of King's Ripton, 1627–32; Archdeacon of Coventry, 1631. He published a tract on the Thirty-nine Articles, and in 1630, he was encouraged to complete a treatise on predestination by Archbishop Laud.[140] He was Archdeacon of Coventry for the last four months of his life and died on 16 September 1632. He was buried in Trinity College Chapel, Cambridge, without monument or epitaph.

---

[138] The ODNB notes: 'On 23 February 1622 the king presented him to the rectory of Hemingford Abbots, Huntingdonshire, of which he had long had promise.' It is not clear how this is to be reconciled with the institution record, which lists the patron as 'Chroferus [i.e. Christopherus] Brooke'. CCEd.

[139] ODNB, *ibid*.

[140] *De Natura & Ordine divinae Praedestinationis in Ecclesia, vel intra Ecclesiam Dei.* Trinity College Cambridge MS B.15.13. Publication was prevented, owing to a general prohibition on debating the subject.

Reign of Charles I (1625–49)

Peter Heylyn, Rector (1631)

Patron: The Crown (Charles I)

Figure 23 Peter Heylyn

Peter Heylyn [variant Heylin] was born on 29 November 1599 in Burford, Oxfordshire, the son of Henry Heylyn and Elizabeth Clampard[141].

---

[141] See https://en.wikipedia.org/wiki/Peter_Heylyn and https://doi.org/10.1093/ref:odnb/13171. 'Theologo-Historicus, or, The True Life of the Most Reverend Divine, and Excellent Historian, Peter Heylyn ... Written by His Son in Law, John Barnard ... to Correct the Errors, Supply the Defects, and Confute the Calumnies

He married Letitia Highgate and had a large family. He entered the Merchant Taylors' School in 1612, and at 14, went to Hart Hall, Oxford. Matriculating at Magdalen College, Oxford in 1616, aged 16, as a Demy or foundation scholar, he graduated BA in 1617. Elected a Fellow in 1618, he gained his MA in 1620. He lectured on historical geography, and in 1621 his lectures were published as *MIKPOKOΣMOΣ: A Little Description of the Great World*. Eight editions were published between 1621 and 1639. He was a prolific author, with twenty-one publications listed in his Wikipedia entry, some of which link with the sequestrations[142] described by Dr John Walker and the later Rector Robert Hanbury.

At Magdalen, Heylyn was dubbed 'the perpetual dictator', as 'impositor' of the Hall. He was a controversialist and an ardent Royalist. He became an outspoken preacher and one of Charles I's clerical followers. He proceeded Bachelor of Divinity in 1629. He became licensed as a prebendary of Westminster and Rector of Hemingford Abbots, where he was instituted on 17 October 1631, and in the following year was Rector of Houghton-le-Spring, County Durham. He was licensed to preach in 1633, became Rector of Arlesford in Hampshire, proceeded Doctor of Divinity, and became a chaplain to Charles I. Like his predecessor Samuel Brooke, he was in conflict with William Prynne and contributed to his prosecution for sedition. As a canon of Westminster, he was no doubt expected to seek evidence against another of Laud's opponents, the Dean of Westminster. In 1639, he became Rector at South Warnborough in Hampshire.[143] He was deprived of his preferments under the Commonwealth and settled at Lacies Court in Abingdon. At the Restoration of Charles II, Heylyn was made Sub-Dean of Westminster but was in

of a Late Writer; Also an Answer to Mr. Baxters False Accusations of Dr. Heylyn.' https://quod.lib.umich.edu/e/eebo/A30989.0001.001?view=toc.

[142] On the legal aspects of sequestration, the seizure of a living, see https://ecclesiasticallaw.wordpress.com/2012/11/17/ecclesiastical-sequestration/.

[143] The full list of his appointments is: 1631 Presentation, Westminster Abbey, Prebendary; 1631 Presentation, Hemingford Abbots, Rector; 1633 Collation, Arlesford, Rector; 1633 Presentation, Houghton-le-Spring, Rector; 1639 Dispensation, South Warnborough, Rector; 1639 Dispensation, King Charles / royal chaplain in ordinary; 1639 Institution, South Warnborough, Rector; 1639 Dispensation, Arlesford, Rector; 1642 Liber cleri, South Warneborow, Rector; 1642 Liber cleri, Arlesford Nova, Rector. CCEd 107125.

poor health. He died on 8 May 1662, and his monument is in Westminster Abbey, where he was buried.[144]

Figure 24 Peter Heylyn's monument, Westminster Abbey

[144] A translation of the inscription is provided by his son-in-law: 'A Monument of Mortality. Of Peter *Heylyn* Doctor of Divinity. Prebendary and Sub-Dean of this Church. A man truly worthy of remembrance. Endowed with excellent parts. Of a sharp and pregnant Wit. A solid and clear Judgement. A memory tenacious to a Miracle. Whereunto he added an incredible Patience in Study. And therein still persisted, when his Eye sight ceased. He Writ many Books, upon various subjects, (that are now in mens hands), containing in them nothing thats Vulgar either for Style or Argument. On all occasions he was a constant Assertor of the Churches Right and the King's Prerogative, as well in their afflicted as prosperous estate. Also he was a severe and vigorous opposer of Rebels and Schismaticks. A despiser of Envy, and a man of undaunted Spirit. While he was seriously intent on these, and many more like Studies Death commanded him to be silent, but could not silence his Fame. *He died in the Sixty third year of his Age.*' John Barnard, *Theologo-Historicus, Or, The True Life of the Most Reverend Divine and Excellent Historian Peter Heylyn, D.D., Sub-Dean of Westminster: Also an Answer to Mr. Baxters False Accusations of Dr. Heylyn* (Printed for J.S. ..., 1683), pp. 294–95. Cf. https://en.wikipedia.org/wiki/John_Barnard_(biographer).

Figure 25 Μικροκοσμος by Peter Heylyn, 1629

Theodore Crowley, Rector (1632)

Patron: Robert Paige

Theodore Crowley [variant Crawley] was instituted on 11 January 1632,[145] but on 22 October 1632, he had already resigned. He was born c. 1587, in Lombard Street, London, received his BA from Christ's College, Cambridge in 1607/8 and his MA in 1611. He was ordained deacon and priest on 8 March 1612. He held appointments as Curate of St Ann Blackfriars (1612); St Paul and All Saints, Bedford (1618); Preacher throughout

---

[145] CCEd. Cf. also *Calendar of the Docquets of Lord Keeper Coventry 1625–40*, Volumes 34–35, p. 142, for 5 November 1631 'Theodor Crowley, M.A. may hold vicarage of St. Paul & All Saints, Bedford with rectory of Hemingford Abbots (Lincoln)'.

the diocese of Lincoln (1631); Rector of Hemingford Abbots (11/01/1632 – 22/10/1632); Rector of Bedford St John, with mastership of St John's Hospital, Bedford, annexed (1663).[146] The patronage of the Mastership and Rectory of St. John's Hospital and Church in Bedford was vested in the Corporation. The roles of Master and Rector were sequestrated in 1653. The Corporation appointed John Gifford, the Minister of Mill Street Chapel. Theodore Rowley was subsequently reinstated and served until his death on 16 October 1663.[147]

Simeon Paige, Rector (1632–69)

Patrons: Robert Paige, Sr and Robert Paige, Jr

Simeon Paige[148] was the son of John Paige, Gent. He was born at Hemingford Abbots, c. 1604–08.[149] John was the brother of Robert Paige, Sr, the lord of the manor. He matriculated in October 1626 at Trinity College, Cambridge, becoming a scholar in 1627.[150] He graduated BA in 1630/1 and proceeded MA in 1634. He was instituted as Rector of Hemingford Abbots on 23 October 1632 and died in post on 5 May 1669, making him one of the longest-serving incumbents (36.5 years).[151]

The patron, Robert Page, Sr died in 1639. His son, Robert Page, Jr, a Royalist, was in dispute with his tenants in 1641.[152] Petitions against

---

[146] 'See https://venn.lib.cam.ac.uk/.

[147] 'Reports and Papers of the Architectural and Archaeological Societies of the Counties of Lincoln and Northampton.', *Associated Architectural Societies' Reports and Papers*, vol. 16 (1891), p. 93.

[148] Paige was the usual spelling of the surname, though Page is also found. Simeon is mostly found in the ecclesiastical records, though Symon and Simon are found in other documents. See CCEd.

[149] The Register of Baptisms for 1604–5 is damaged but shows that a son of John Paige was baptized in February 1605.

[150] This would normally presuppose a date of birth c. 1608. Cf. https://venn.lib.cam.ac.uk/.

[151] CCEd.

[152] See https://discovery.nationalarchives.gov.uk/details/r/9736c5b4-158e-4a7d-8965-9ac8875d4780.

Robert Page, Jr and Simeon Page[153] were presented in 1643 but were op-posed by a counter-petition. Although Simeon Paige was petitioned against on charges of drunkenness and insufficiency, McCall observes that 'the real target was his enclosing cousin Robert, Lord of the Manor'.[154]

The turbulent and divisive times of the Civil War were difficult for all, especially the clergy. Some families became divided, and men were serving in the armies instead of carrying out their usual occupations. There were few local skirmishes, other than the siege of Huntingdon in 1645 and near St Neots three years later, but it is likely that the church was stripped of images and valuables.[155]

Hemingford Abbots may have taken action during the autumn of 1643 or during the previous decade. It is feasible that, when Lord of the Manor, Robert Paige, became patron in 1631, he, or subsequently his son, did not support the Laudian sympathies of the previous rectors Brooke and Heylin. Robert Paige appointed Theodore Crowley and within a year his nephew Simeon Paige, who had recently graduated at the age of 27.

In the eleven years between Simeon Paige's appointment and the 1643 ordinance he would have needed to clarify his churchmanship and politics in relation to his patrons (uncle, then cousin) and the area, in-cluding his near contemporary the Earl of Manchester at

---

[153] 'Pray for the removal of Mr Paige and the settling of a conscionable minister in his place.' (*ibid.*).

[154] Fiona McCall, *Baal's Priests: The Loyalist Clergy and the English Revolution* (London: Routledge, 2016), pp. 95f.

[155] Parliament passed an ordinance on 28 August 1643 that a list of items consid-ered as iconoclastic should be destroyed by All Saints' Day in November. The Earl of Manchester, Parliamentary Commissioner for the Eastern Association, signed a warrant on 19 December 1643 for William Dowsing to enforce the ordi-nance. Dowsing and his soldiers trashed 133 churches in Cambridgeshire but did not visit 69 parishes north of Cambridge. Chris Dunn questioned: 'Was this because the north part of the county has always traditionally been, by and large, Cromwell country and uninfected by "popish innovations"? … The 1643 ordi-nance restricted the "reformation" to innovations introduced "within twenty years last past".' Chris Dunn, in: *Cambridgeshire Life*, February 2002, pp. 47–49.

Hinchingbrooke. Manchester resigned from public life during the 1650s, and they both welcomed the restoration of the monarchy in 1660.

Records were not kept of Oliver Cromwell's activities in this area, unlike the regulations during later despoliation in Suffolk and Norfolk. It is reputed that a hole in the north-western beam of Hemingford Abbots church was caused by a musket ball intended for one of the carved angels.

The episcopal government of the Church was abolished on 9 April 1646, and the Church's lands and properties were confiscated by the state. Gray comments: 'The Church of England officially ceased to exist from 9th February 1649 when the oaths of allegiance, supremacy and canonical obedience incumbent upon all clergymen taking up any office had been abolished.'[156] The re-establishment of the church came with the restoration of the monarchy in 1660. A new Bishop of Lincoln, Robert Sanderson, was consecrated in Westminster Abbey on 28 October.[157]

The living of Hemingford Abbots had been sequestrated for two months, during which Paige had suffered the loss of payment of tithes,[158] which may have strengthened his determination to pursue several parishioners for non-payment of tithes between 1659 and 1663.[159] He petitioned the House of Lords for restitution of tithes in 1660.[160] He was confirmed as Rector, following the Act of Uniformity in 1662, as he

---

[156] Alan Richardson, *The Ecclesiastical Peculiars of Huntingdonshire, 1660–1852* (Huntingdon: Just Print IT!, 2007), p. 15.

[157] *Ibid.*, p. 16.

[158] There were two sorts of tithes: Great Tithes were a percentage of crops from the open arable fields; Lesser Tithes were a percentage of other produce, such as chickens, lambs, apples, eggs, etc. By 1700, the tithes had frequently been commuted to money payments. William Franklin, 'Huntingdonshire Fields c. 1660–c. 1750', in: Evelyn Lord, ed., *The Singing Milkmaids: Life in Post-Restoration Huntingdonshire c.1660–c.1750* (Cambridge: EAH Press, 2019), p. 101.

[159] Liz Ford, 'The Clergy in Post-Restoration Huntingdonshire and the Hearth Tax', in: *The Singing Milkmaids*, p. 177; William Arthur Shaw, *A History of the English Church during the Civil Wars and under the Commonwealth, 1640–1660, Vol. 1* (London: Longmans, Green, and Co, 1900), p. 314.

[160] Cf. https://venn.lib.cam.ac.uk/. Tithes were not paid to him between 1659 and 1663 by John Mason, John Basely and others (Court papers at Hunts Archives AH4/251/44 papers 1–7).

subscribed to the Thirty-nine Articles and agreed to conform with the revised Book of Common Prayer.[161] This Act had the effect of outlawing as nonconformist 'Dissenters' those Puritans who could not accept Anglicanism as defined by the Act.[162] The suppression of dissent was tightened a couple of years later and in 1670 by the Conventicle Acts that banned illegal religious assemblies. Meanwhile, Paige held on to the Rectory until his death in 1669. Considering the fluctuations in churchmanship during his thirty-six and a half years in the post of rector, it was remarkable that seventeen of these were during the reign of Charles I (1632–49), eleven were during the Commonwealth (1649–60), and nine were during the reign of Charles II (1660–69).

The Commonwealth (declared 19 May 1649)

No appointments were made.

Oliver Cromwell, Lord Protector (1653–58)

No appointments were made.

Richard Cromwell, Lord Protector (1658–59)

No appointments were made.

---

[161] Archdeaconry Records, Lincoln Subscription Book III 1662–77–78, folder 16. He signed the Oath of Non-Resistance designed to strengthen the commitment of the clergy to the restored King and Church.

[162] Simon Clemmow, 'Dissent in Post-Restoration Huntingdonshire', in: Evelyn Lord, ed., *The Singing Milkmaids: Life in Post-Restoration Huntingdonshire c.1660–c.1750* (Cambridge: EAH Press, 2019) p. 189.

Reign of Charles II (1660–85)

Thomas Edmonds, Rector (1669)

Patron: Sir John Barnard, 2nd Baronet.

Nine years after the restoration of the monarchy, Thomas Edmonds was appointed rector on 5 May 1669.[163] He was ordained priest by Thomas Whithern on 14 February 1660. His will is dated 15 December 1669, and probate was granted to Edward Hanbury in January 1670.[164] A Thomas Edmonds was appointed Rector of Tingewick, Buckinghamshire on 9 March 1670.[165] In the CCEd, this Edmonds is distinct from the Edmonds who was at Hemingford Abbots.[166]

Edmonds is not listed among the Rectors of Hemingford Abbots and presumably died before taking up the appointment. Robert Hanbury was subsequently Rector of Hemingford Abbots in 1688.

John Rowley, Rector (1669–88)

Patron: Sir John Barnard, 2nd Baronet

Rowley was Rector from c. 1669 until his death on 10 December 1688. He was admitted from a school in Luton to Peterhouse Cambridge as a sizar, aged 18 in 1651. He graduated BA in 1654, MA in 1658. He subscribed the Act of Supremacy in Hemingford Abbots as Rector. No date is recorded.[167] The following appointments are recorded: 1662 Licensing, Diocese of Lincoln as Preacher; 1663, Houghton cum Wyton. He was Vicar of Brampton, Huntingdonshire from 1664 to 1688. He was aged about 36 when he was also appointed to Hemingford Abbots[168] and served for nineteen years until his death.[169]

---

[163] CCEd; Archdeaconry Records, Lincoln.

[164] http://www.winslow-history.org.uk/winslow_will_edmunds1670.shtm.

[165] National Archives PROB 11/332/25

[166] CCEd Person IDs: 88073 and 88074.

[167] CCEd.

[168] Induction Mandate; Hunts Archives AH26/234 paper 22.

[169] https://venn.lib.cam.ac.uk/.

The Hearth Tax records provide a useful description of the size and quantity of houses in the parish between 1662 and 1689.[170] This tax of two shillings per annum was levied to support the royal household. In the first couple of years, it was refined in England to focus on the occupiers of properties with more than two hearths. The abolition of this tax was a popular element in the 'Glorious Revolution' of 1688.

Some of the challenges facing Rowley can be clarified by considering the national context of the Church of England and its treatment of Dissenters. The persecution of Protestant nonconformists and Roman Catholics nationally after the Conventicle Acts was ameliorated to some extent by the 1672 Declaration of Indulgence. This allowed Catholics to worship privately and Protestants to license ministers and meeting houses. Baptist churches were granted licences in Fenstanton, Godmanchester and St Ives.[171] However, this was short-lived, and governmental attitudes hardened again subsequently.

The Hearth Tax records of 1674 and the 'Compton Census' of religious affiliation two years later indicated that the proportion of Dissenters in the population in Huntingdonshire was only about 5%.[172] The 'strength of dissent' in Hemingford Abbots can be shown by the percentage of dissenters in the population of the village.[173] The raw numbers of dissenters in these adjacent villages on the south side of the Ouse valley add up to a proportion that was more than double the county average.

---

[170] Hearth Tax Digital: Huntingdonshire (forthcoming). https://www.roehampton.ac.uk/Research-Centres/Centre-for-Hearth-Tax-Research/.

[171] *Minutes of the General Assembly of the General Baptist Churches in England: With Kindred Records, Edited with Introduction and Notes for the Baptist Historical Society, by W. T. Whitley.* (London: Printed for the Society by the Kingsgate Press, 1909), vol. 1, 1654–1728, p. lix, quoted in Clemmow, p. 204.

[172] However the ambiguities in the census statistics have been explored by Anne Whiteman and Mary Clapinson in: *The Compton Census of 1676: A Critical Edition, Edited by Anne Whiteman with the Assistance of Mary Clapinson,* Records of Social and Economic History; New Ser., 10 (London: Oxford University Press for the British Academy, 1986) and subsequently by Alasdair Crockett and K.D.M. Snell, 'From the 1676 Compton Census to the 1851 Census of Religious Worship: Religious Continuity or Discontinuity?', *Rural History,* 8.1 (1997), 55–89. Quoted by Clemmow, pp. 192–208.

[173] These figures and several insights are extended in Clemmow, pp. 197–208.

Place	Conformists	Dissenters	Strength of Dissent
Godmanchester	736	65	8.10%
Hemingford Abbots	136	50	26.90%
Hemingford Grey	191	17	8.20%
Fenstanton	286	39	12.00%

Only Ellington (27.3% of 80) and Grafham (24.1% of 85) also recorded over 20% in Huntingdonshire. However, it is likely that several factors combined to result in there being more dissent in Hemingford Abbots during Rowley's time than in most of the other ninety-three parishes in the county. Rowley held the living in plurality and probably lived in Brampton. He followed Simeon Page, who had died after thirty-six and a half years formally in post. The parish needed leadership in the 1670s, and Rowley was less likely to have been effective as a part-timer living so far out of the village.

The Hearth Tax returns indicate that Hemingford Abbots, though smaller, had a higher proportion of houses with several hearths than most neighbouring villages. Forty-four percent had three or more hearths, as compared with an average of eighteen percent across Huntingdonshire.[174] Where house size indicated superior socio-economic status, the potential links with a higher level of literacy, independence of thought, and potential reaction to enforced conformism could have been reinforced by a sense of vacuum of leadership in the parish church. Perhaps the situation began to improve with the licensing of John Slater as

[174] Huntingdonshire Hearth Tax Assessments 1674 PRO E/179/249/2 Hunts Archives 1992; T. Arkell, 'Identifying Regional Variations from the Hearth Tax', *The Local Historian*, 33 no 3 (August 2003), p. 156; Clemmow, p. 206.

Curate in 1680.[175] The first records of excommunication in the parish date from 1684.[176]

It appears that discontent about the payment of tithes and the Church Rate during and after Commonwealth times had strengthened into dissent, as the nonconformists gained momentum despite persecution. There is evidence of a 'descent of dissent' through generations and across the social spectrum.[177]

The charismatic Henry Denne had founded the Calvinist Particular Baptist churches in Fenstanton and Warboys in the 1640s and 1650s, and these continued to attract members from the surrounding parishes.[178] In Fenstanton and Hemingford Grey, the Constables and Ministers were bound over in 1668 for 'allowing unlawful conventicles'. In 1679, Tobias Hardmeat, John Offley, and John Gray of Fenstanton were sent to the assizes for not attending church but attending Quaker meetings.[179] The Quakers acquired a burial ground in Godmanchester in 1672 and built a meeting house in about 1685. Hardmeat was sent to prison for a least a year in 1683 for refusing to pay tithes. Rowley and the incumbents of neighbouring churches needed to attract active support for the Established Church rather than mere compliance in the context of such alternatives.

[175] Archdeaconry Records, Lincoln

[176] The excommunication of Roger Ingram and Maria Cole. Huntingdon Record Office AH12/26/267/78.

[177] Margaret Spufford, *Contrasting Communities English Villages in the Sixteenth and Seventeenth Centuries* (Cambridge: University Press, 1979), pp. 300–06, quoted in Clemmow, p. 192.

[178] *Records of the Churches of Christ, Gathered at Fenstanton, Warboys, and Hexham, 1644–1720, edited for the Hanserd Knollys Society, by Edward Bean Underhill.* (London: Printed for the Society, by Haddon Brothers, 1854), pp. vii–viii, quoted in Clemmow, p. 200.

[179] Jack Dady, *Beyond Yesterday: A History of Fenstanton*, Millennium ed. (Fenstanton: Archival Books, 2002), pp. 62, 66, 81.

John Slater, Curate (1680)

Slater was ordained deacon on 19 September 1680 and took up the curacy of Hemingford Abbots on 20 September 1680. He held the degree of BA.

William Dickons, Preacher (1687)

William Dickons [Dickens], MA, was ordained deacon on 19 September 1686 and priest on 18 December 1687. He came to Hemingford Abbots as a preacher on 19 December 1687. John Rowley died on 10 December 1688 and was succeeded by Robert Hanbury. William Dickons was instituted as Rector of Boxworth in 1690 and died in post on 23 December 1707.[180]

Reign of James II (1685–88)

Robert Hanbury, Rector (1688–1712)

Patron: Sir Robert Bernard, 3rd Baronet

Robert Hanbury was the son of John Hanbury, of Ottery St Mary, Devon, Gent. He matriculated at St Mary Hall, Oxford, on 14 March 1667/8, aged 17 and received the degree of Bachelor of Civil Law from Hart Hall, Oxford. He held the following posts: rector of Long Newnton Wilts, 1676; vicar of Leatherhead, Surrey, 1679–1712; rector of Hemingford Abbatis, 1688–1712, and rector of Denton, Hunts, 1707–1712. He was licensed at Hemingford Abbots as rector and preacher on 10 December 1688.[181]

There are nine Deeds of Excommunication and three Penances for adultery and defamation in the Huntingdon Record Office relating to parishioners of Hemingford Abbots during Robert Hanbury's incumbency. Records of the Baptist Chapel at Fenstanton from 1676 mention members from the Hemingfords, Godmanchester, and St Ives.

Parish Records of Baptisms, Marriages and Burials survive from 1690/3. Earlier Bishops' Transcripts record original Registers, now lost, for most years between 1604 and 1625.

---

[180] See https://venn.lib.cam.ac.uk/; CCEd 14895

[181] *Alumni Oxonienses, 1500–1714*, p. 642; CCEd 152935.

Other archives from Robert Hanbury's incumbency include a Terrier of the Glebe Land, Poor Rate Assessments, the Vestry Minute Book, and Bishop's Transcripts of Registers. There are also records of his drinking problem. He was in trouble with the Church authorities in 1698 for 'excessive drinking and neglect of duty' and in 1707, when he was accused by William Maxey of 'excessive drinking, irreverent reading and of curtailing the service of the Church etc.' He was admonished by the Bishop to take care to avoid any scandal in the future.

He corresponded with the publisher Robert Clavell of the Peacock in Paternoster Row, London on 30 August 1705, giving information about Simeon Paige, a predecessor of his as Rector of Hemingford Abbots, who died in 1669.

In 1706, following Sir Robert Bernard's death, the advowson passed to his son, Sir John Bernard.[182] The moiety of the Manor was sold to Cornelius Denne, a merchant. His relationship if any to the dissenter Henry Denne, who had died in 1661, is not clear. However, in the generation between the Compton census of 1676 and Wake's Visitations of 1706–12, the strength of dissent in Hemingford Abbots had declined from 26.9% to 4.9%.[183] In 1706, three Baptist and three Quaker families were recorded among the fifty to sixty-nine families in the parish (10.9%). In 1709, there were twenty-one Dissenters among the 250 inhabitants (8.4%) and in 1712, one Baptist and two Quaker families among sixty-one (4.9%).

This significant shift in dissent from the incumbency of Rowley to that of Hanbury may be due to his effectiveness, helped by the appointment of a curate, Thomas Whishaw, in 1709. Hanbury lived in the Parsonage House at Hemingford Abbots, although he held two other parishes in plurality. The Toleration Act of 1689 replaced the persecution of Dissenters with the right to worship, and this national change of attitude after the 'Glorious Revolution' of William and Mary also helped. Hanbury died in post on 27 January 1712.

The death of parishioner Professor Joshua Barnes (1654–1712) occurred in the same year. His memorial in the chancel includes a lyrical epitaph in Greek: 'Barnes outdid all men as a polymath, best of writers in prose, flower of bards, greatest of inquirers (historians?), best of

---

[182] See above, pp. 23f.
[183] Clemmow, p. 203.

orators, deepest of seers of British land.'[184] However, Barnes's main claim to remembrance rests on his imposing contribution to medieval history, *History of That Most Victorious Monarch, Edward IIId* (1688),[185] not on his work as a Greek scholar or a divine.[186]

Figure 26 Barnes monument

[184] Translated by Dr Anthony Bowen.

[185] *The History of That Most Victorious Monarch, Edward IIId, King of England and France, and Lord of Ireland, and First Founder of the Most Noble Order of the Garter: Being a Full and Exact Account of the Life and Death of the Said King: Together with That of His Most Renowned Son, Edward, Prince of Wales and of Aquitain, Sirnamed the Black-Prince: Faithfully and Carefully Collected from the Best and Most Antient Authors, Domestick and Foreign, Printed Books, Manuscripts and Records / by Joshua Barnes.* (Cambridge: Printed by John Hayes for the author, 1688).

[186] Hunts Archives AH26/235/32 & Bishop's Reg 36 p. 57, sub book 6A, p. 42 (1707). See also Michael T. Cherniavsky, 'Joshua Barnes Historian', in: *7 Short Pieces* (privately printed, 1984). The school Barnes had attended in Horsham, Christ's Hospital, has a boarding house named after him. The sundial over its front door reads 'Umbra fugit, manet res'—'The shadow flies, the situation (things) remains.'

Reign of William III (1689–1702) and Mary II (1689–94)

No appointments were made.

Reign of Anne (1702–14)

Thomas Whishaw, Curate (1709)

Thomas Whishaw, a BA of Brasenose College, Oxford was licensed on 26 September 1709. He remained for only one year, leaving for a curacy in Swineshead in Lincolnshire on 31 August 1710. He became vicar of Salford, Bedfordshire, 1713; rector of Gt Munden, Hertfordshire, 1718–56; Precentor of Hereford, 1722–56; Canon 1723–53; Canon of Sarum, 1727–56, and of Winchester, 1739–56. He died in 1756.[187]

John Smith, Rector (1712–13)

Patron: Sir John Bernard, 4th Baronet

As the patron was aged 17, his widowed mother, Lady Anna Trevor, was involved in the appointment of John Smith, who was instituted on 21 January 1712.[188] Smith was admitted to Jesus College, Cambridge as a sizar in 1690, matriculated in 1691 and appointed Rustat Scholar in 1692. He graduated BA in 1694/5 and took his MA in 1698. Ordained deacon in 1708 by the Bishop of Lincoln in Westminster Abbey, he was ordained priest in 1709.[189] His first parish was Hundleby with Stickney in Lincolnshire, then Great Stukeley in Huntingdonshire. This was an unattractive parish, and Smith reported to Bishop Wake's Visitation in 1712 that 'He has to have another parish, where he resides, because his living is so

---

[187] https://venn.lib.cam.ac.uk/.

[188] CCEd.

[189] Lincoln Bishop's Reg 36 pp 60 & 101 Sub book 6A pp. 45f.

poor.'[190] Sixty-one families lived in Hemingford Abbots at the time.[191] He died on 20 September 1713 and was buried on 2 May 1714.[192]

Reign of George I (1714–27)

Alexander Burrell, Rector (1714)

Patron: Sir John Bernard, 4th Baronet

Noble lists Alexander Burrell under 1714; however, there is no entry in the CCEd under Hemingford Abbots. Two Alexander Burrells are listed in the CCEd: Person IDs 5067 and 5068. Venn lists R. of Hemingford Abbots, [Huntingdonshire], in 1714 for 'Alexander BURREL; Approx. lifespan: 1687–1771; Adm. pens. (age 15) at Trinity College 1702:07:11'.[193] Assuming this is correct, the following biography is possible: Alexander Burrell [variants Burrel and Burwell] graduated BA at Trinity College Cambridge in 1706/7. He was ordained Deacon in 1710 and Priest in 1710, when he also gained his MA. After serving as college chaplain, he was Vicar of Buckden from 1713 to 1720. In 1714, he was Rector of Hemingford Abbots while Samuel Dickens was a deacon. He was a Prebendary of Lincoln from 1717 and from 1720 was Rector of Adstock in Buckinghamshire (until 1762) and of Puttenham in Hertfordshire until his death in 1771. It was normal at this time for prebendaries

---

[190] John Broad, ed., *Bishop Wake's Summary of Visitation Returns from the Diocese of Lincoln 1706–15*, Part 2: Huntingdonshire, Hertfordshire (Part), Bedfordshire, Leicestershire, Buckinghamshire, Records of Social and Economic History (Oxford, New York: Oxford University Press, 2013), p. 525, n. 69, quoted in Clemmow p. 180, n.116.

[191] See Appendix, pp. 177ff., below.

[192] There is a monument in the sanctuary under the carpet giving his date of death, which is quoted in 'Monumental Inscriptions in the Parish Church and Churchyard of St Margaret of Antioch', Hemingford Abbots, *Huntingdonshire Family History Society* 1991 (typescript).

[193] See https://venn.lib.cam.ac.uk.

and parochial clergy to hold one or several livings in addition to the prebend and any cathedral and archdeaconry roles.[194]

Samuel Dickens, Deacon (1713), Rector (1714–48)

Patron: Sir John Bernard, 4th Baronet

Samuel Dickens [variant Dicken] was born in 1690, the son of Joseph Dickens, a cutler of Birmingham. He matriculated at Brasenose College, Oxford on 20 March 1706/7, aged 16, graduating BA in 1710. He was ordained deacon in Christchurch Cathedral, Oxford in 1711 and was married to Mary Hildersley on 21 July 1713 by his uncle, Nathaniel Gower. He was licensed and appointed deacon at Hemingford Abbots on 14 August 1713 and ordained priest at Peterborough on 18 September 1714. He was instituted at Hemingford Abbots by Alexander Burrell, Vicar of Buckden and Domestic Chaplain to Bishop William Wake of Lincoln acting as his Commissary, 20 Sept 1714. He received his BA (Oxon.) from Brasenose in 1710 and had an MA from King's College, Cambridge in 1719.[195]

Seven of his ten children survived to adulthood and were born between 1717 and 1726: Samuel II (1717–91) became Archdeacon of Durham; Charles (1719–93) followed his father as incumbent in the Hemingfords; Thomas (1721–89) became a Lieutenant-Colonel in the Guards; Catherine (b. 1726) married Thomas Hazelwood, and their son, Canon Dickens Hazelwood, became Vicar of Aycliffe, County Durham.

Ten years after coming to Hemingford Abbots, Samuel Dickens was also inducted as Vicar of Hemingford Grey, on 2 May 1724. The Terriers describing the Glebe land in 1724 and a century later in 1822 are at Lincoln. Excommunications continued while he was responsible for both parishes. There were two Quakers, an Anabaptist and at least thirteen

---

[194] 'Pluralism was regulated by an Act of Henry VIII (21 Hen VIII c.13) which permitted clergy who were chaplains to the aristocracy or others to hold livings in plurality. The act which sought to regulate pluralism cancelled out any good by the clauses allowing plurality of livings ... No-one could effectively look after such responsibilities often miles apart. This problem was solved by livings being filled by ill-paid curates and the evil of the non-resident clergyman was perpetuated.' Richardson, pp. 17ff. https://en.wikipedia.org/wiki/Prebendary.

[195] See https://venn.lib.cam.ac.uk; CCEd13203.

paupers living in Hemingford Abbots in 1717–20 among the fifty-five families. Dickens served as a surrogate for the Commissary Judge in the Archdeaconry Court of Huntingdon from 1727 to 1745.

Dickens and his son held the incumbencies of Hemingford Abbots and Hemingford Grey from 1724 to 1793, being the second and third priests to do so. Dickens was assisted for several of the years between 1727 and 1748 by a succession of three deacons and two curates, including his son Charles. They fit the picture of the 'growing professionalism of a clergy who set an example to their parishioners, paid attention to their flocks and encouraged regular church attendance'.[196]

When his son succeeded him at Hemingford Grey in 1744, the year in which his wife died, Samuel was inducted as Rector of Houghton with Wyton and served there until his death, four years later, on 11 April 1748. Samuel Dickens was buried in Wyton churchyard (floor stone). There is a stained-glass memorial at Hemingford Abbots at the east end of the north aisle.

Figure 27 Dickens window

[196] Nigel Yates, *Eighteenth Century Britain: Religion and Politics 1714–1815* (London: Routledge, 2014), pp. 130–42. https://doi.org/10.4324/9781315834979.

George Barber, Deacon (1727)

He was born c. 1705, gained a BA from St John's College, Cambridge (1725/6), ordained deacon on 28 May 1727 and licensed in Hemingford Abbots on 29 May 1727. He was ordained priest on 21 September 1729 and then served as a curate in Ampthill, possibly becoming perpetual curate of Tarleton, Lancashire, 1746–65.[197] He died c. 1765.

Reign of George II (1727–60)

Henry Nicholls, Deacon (1731)

This is most likely Henry Nicholls, from Chilham in Kent, b. c. 1708, he was a scholar at Trinity Hall 1726/7, who received his LLB (Cantab.) in 1731 and was ordained deacon on 14 June 17.[198] He died c. 1806.

John Williamson, Deacon (1732)

John Williamson, who was born, c. 1709, came from Liverpool, was a scholar at Trinity Hall in 1727/8 and proceeded LLB in 1731. He was ordained deacon on 4 June 1732 and priest on 3 September 1732. He was licensed at Hemingford Abbots on 5 June 1732.[199] He died c. 1806.

Charles Powlett, Curate (1739)

Charles Powlett [variant Pawlett] was born, c. 1718 in London and went to school in Ireland. He was a pensioner at Trinity College, Cambridge (1736), then a scholar (1737). Ordained deacon on 23 September 1739 and priest on 20 January1739/40, he was licensed as curate at Hemingford Abbots on 24 September 1739. He may have been chaplain in the Navy, 1739–43. He died c. 1816.[200]

---

[197] CCEd; https://venn.lib.cam.ac.uk/.
[198] CCEd; https://venn.lib.cam.ac.uk/.
[199] CCEd; https://venn.lib.cam.ac.uk/.
[200] CCEd; https://venn.lib.cam.ac.uk/.

Charles Dickens, Curate (1744–48), Rector (1748–93)

Patron: Sir John Bernard, 4th Baronet

Charles Dickens was born in 1720, the second son of the previous rector, Samuel Dickens. He was baptized at Hemingford Abbots on 17 June 1720. Educated at Charterhouse, London. Exhibitioner. Matriculated 1739. Admitted as Scholar at Trinity Hall Cambridge 7 January 1740. LLB 1745, LLD 1767.[201]

Ordained Deacon at Buckden, 20 May 1744 by John Thomas, Bishop of Lincoln to the Cure of Hemingford Grey 21 May 1744. Ordained Priest at Peterborough 11 June 1744. Rector of Hemingford Grey 1744–1793. Instituted to the Vicarage of Hemingford Grey, in the gift of Trinity College, Cambridge. He was instituted as curate of Hemingford Abbots on 21 May 1744.

On his father's death Charles succeeded him as Rector of Hemingford Abbots from 1748 until his own death in 1793. Induction, 19 July 1748. Married Mary Strachan 19 December 1750 at St Benet, Gracechurch, London.

On 18 May 1748, the Archdeacon of Huntingdon, Timothy Neve, noted in Hemingford Abbots Church that 'the chancel was much out of repair' and 'two bells cracked, to be re-run'. Five bells were installed in 1754, the sixth being added in 1897. They were re-hung in 1994 and continue to be rung regularly. Archdeacon Neve also criticised the state of the churchyard, the roof, walls and the Rectory.[202]

---

[201] CCEd; https://venn.lib.cam.ac.uk/.

[202] 'Plough and rubbish to be removed; basin for ye font; walls to be cleaned and plaistered and whitewashed. Elders and rubbish round ye church to be cut down. Chancel much out of repair and ordered to be cleared. Both roof, cover, wells and buttresses to be secured and made decent. House etc greatly dilapidated and ordered to be sufficiently repaired.' Alan Richardson, 'The tour of the Rev Timothy Neve DD through the Archdeaconry of Huntingdon May–July 1748', *Records of Huntingdonshire*, 2 (1987).

Figure 28 Memorial to Mary Dickens

In 1761, divine service at Hemingford Abbots took place twice on the Lord's Day, Catechising in Lent, Communion four times. At Hemingford Grey, divine service took place once on the Lord's Day and on festival days, Catechising in Lent, and often at other times. At Houghton with Wyton, divine service once on the Lord's Day at each church, Communion 3 times at least, Catechising in Lent and at other times.[203]

In December 1748, 'A vault and pew over it at the east end of the north aisle was erected by the widow Huske with the consent of the Minister and Churchwardens.'[204] She was buried 20 years later, on 24 June

---

[203] 'Speculum Dioceseos Sub Episcopo Johanne Thomas A.D. 1744–61', pp. 177–79; see https://www.lincstothepast.com/Speculum-Dioceseos-sub-episcopo-Johanne-Thomas-A-D--1744-61/722087.record?pt=S.

[204] *Miscellany of Extracts from the Register, Vestry Book, and PCC Minutes, 1688–1950*, compiled by several rectors of St Margaret's [manuscript, c. 1950, in private collection].

1768. The vault was empty when discovered by heating engineers in 1948.

He was appointed prebendary of Hatherton at Wolverhampton collegiate church on 12 November 1763[205], and in 1768 and 1778 he was installed to responsibilities in Lincoln Diocese.[206] Curates were appointed in 1769, Thomas Roger Filewood; 1780, John Hopkins; 1781, William Gunsley Ayerst; and 1789, William Cowling.

Unfortunately, these dates coincide with gaps in the registers. There appear to be no records of baptisms between March 1769 and October 1778; of marriages between 1764 and 1797; or of burials between 1769 and 1778, or between 1779 and 1793. It is not known whether such events took place but were not recorded appropriately; or were recorded elsewhere; or were diverted to other parishes. It may be even that successive curates presumed that such records were kept by the Rector or Churchwardens. One effect of these gaps has been to create difficulties in tracing continuity in family histories.

In 1772 he was put under a subpoena to appear at the Quarter Sessions on 6th October concerning the relationship between the assessment and payment of the Poor Rate and the income from the tithes.[207]

In 1777, Charles Dickens published a sermon occasioned by the death of James Favell, DD, 'preached and inscribed particularly to the parishioners of Houghton and Wyton by Charles Dickens LLD Rector of Hemingford Abbots'. James Favell had been at Sutton in the Marsh in 1755 and was followed there by Charles Dickens in 1778. Charles was installed as Prebendary of Sutton in the Marsh in Lincoln Cathedral on 23 May 1778 [208]. He was also Prebendary of Wolverhampton.

---

[205] CCEd.

[206] 1768 Huntingdon Record Office AH2/248/80, 81 and 1778 Lincoln A/3/15 p. 180, Dean and Chapter Book.

[207] A copy of his defence is among 26 archives relating to Hemingford Abbots between 1630 and 1872 that are in the Norris Museum, St Ives (Alan Richardson to Charles Beresford 11 May 2003).

[208] Lincoln Archives Bishop's Reg 39 p. 301. Dean & Chapter Act Book A/3/15 p. 180. Sub Book 9 fol.177v. The prebendary's induction process of Dickens's contemporary Robert Hodson (1726–1803) of All Saints', Huntingdon is described in Alan Richardson (2006–07) *Hunts Records*, 4 no. 2, pp 15–18. Dickens's experience would have been very similar. (Correspondence with CB 21 March 2018)

In 1785 his youngest daughter Susannah (1760–1833) married Rev Thomas Brown (1761–1829), Rector of Conington and son of Lancelot 'Capability' Brown of Fenstanton. Their two sons were both ordained.[209]

In 1792, there were 50 families in the parish, including 13 paupers. In 1717–20, there had been 2 Quakers and an Anabaptist. [210] In 1792 there were still Quakers. The rental income was £250, the equivalent of £38,000 in 2020. The Rector was resident in the parish.[211] In contrast, the rental income of Sutton in the Marsh was £20, equivalent to £3,000 in 2020.[212]

In 1792, he published 'an occasional, multifarious sermon on the following words of St Paul 'We exhort you, Brethren, warn them that are unruly' by C. Dickens LL.D. Inscribed to Robert Burton Esqr., Cromwell Place, St Ives.'

His obituary notice in the *Gentleman's Magazine* records: 'In 1793, he published 'A Sermon upon the general fast, preached at the two Hemingfords, Huntingdonshire, by the Minister of both parishes on Friday 19th April 1793, by command, and in ready obedience to the powers that be in church and state, occasioned from declaration of just and necessary war against our unprovoked enemies, whose most horrible iniquities and cruelties alarm and astonish the whole world, more especially principalities and powers who are Christian ones. Also one upon our *militia* going forth with alacrity; and another setting forth the *necessity* of keeping holy the *Sabbath day*. For the benefit of the widows and children of the Huntingdonshire unfortunate militia. Printed at Huntingdon.' 4to.'[213]

He died at the Rectory House, Hemingford Abbots, on 27 Sept 1793, aged 74. He was buried at Hemingford Abbots and is commemorated on a monument in the Chancel.

---

[209] Genealogy of Dicken (sic) family in correspondence between CB and Sue Page (née Dickin), 6 May 2016.

[210] *Speculum* 1705–23 p. 283.

[211] *Speculum* 1663–1784 p. 178 and 1788–92, p. 122.

[212] *Speculum* 1663–1784, p. 32.

[213] *The Gentleman's Magazine*, lxiii (2) (F. Jeffries, 1793) https://books.google.co.uk/books?id=PqY2AQAAMAAJ, p. 959.

Figure 29 Memorial to Charles Dickens

Thomas Roger Filewood, Curate (1769)

Thomas Roger Filewood was born, c. 1747 and educated at St John's College, Cambridge, where he was a scholar. He graduated BA in 1769 and MA in 1772. He was licensed as a curate at Hemingford Abbots on 22 May 1769, after having been ordained deacon on 21 May 1769. He was ordained priest on 9 May 1771 and was Rector of Mickleham, Surrey, 1771–1800 and Rector of Dunsfold, [Surrey], 1786–1800. He was also Domestic Chaplain to John Butler, Bishop of Oxford and Hereford (1786). He died in 1800.[214]

[214] CCEd; https://venn.lib.cam.ac.uk/.

John Hopkins, Curate (1780)

John Hopkins was born, c. 1757 in Marston Trussell, Northamptonshire. He was licensed as curate at Hemingford Abbots on 22 May 1780 after his ordination as deacon on 21 May 1780. His education was at Christ's College, Cambridge, where he entered as a sizar in 1774. He became a scholar in 1775 and took his BA in 1779 as 7th Wrangler.[215] He proceeded MA in 1783, became a fellow in 1785, Senior Proctor in 1801. He was ordained priest in 1786. After Hemingford Abbots, he held posts as Curate of Fen Drayton, Cambridgeshire, 1792 and Curate of Luddenham, Kent, in 1809. He died, aged 74, in 1831.[216]

William Gunsley Ayerst, Curate (1781)

William Gunsley Ayerst was born c. 1758. He came from Kent and attended Rochester School, proceeding to Trinity College, Cambridge, where he graduated BA in 1780, MA in 1783. He was ordained deacon on 10 June 1781 and licensed to Hemingford Abbots on 11 June 1781. Ordained priest on 16 March 1783, he became rector of Eastbridge, Kent, 1784–90, and curate of Speldhurst, 1787. He died on 25 September 1790.[217]

William Cowling, Curate (1789)

William Cowling was born, c. 1766 in Fenstanton, Huntingdonshire.[218] He was a pensioner at St John's College, Cambridge, 1784, afterwards a scholar. He took his BA in 1788 and MA in 1791. He was ordained deacon on 7 June 1789 and was licensed as a curate at Hemingford Abbots on the same day. Ordained priest on 13 May 1790, he became Curate of Wicken Bonhunt, Essex, from 1791 and Rector from 1807–14; chaplain to Philip, Earl of Hardwicke, in 1811; vicar of Albury, Hertfordshire, 1811–

---

[215] I.e., the seventh-best candidate in the first class of the Mathematics Tripos.

[216] CCEd; https://venn.lib.cam.ac.uk/.

[217] CCEd; https://venn.lib.cam.ac.uk/.

[218] He was a contemporary of Thomas Brown in childhood in Fenstanton and at St John's, Cambridge. Thomas Brown was a son of Lancelot 'Capability' Brown and married Susannah, the daughter of the Rev. Charles Dickens.

46 and rector of Newton Blossomville, Buckinghamshire, 1814–46. He died in 1846.[219]

Reign of George III (1760–1820)

Thomas Stafford, Rector (1793–97)

Patrons: Rogers Parker, Stanhope Pedley, and John Smith, Trustees under the Will of Sir Robert Bernard, 5th Baronet

Thomas Stafford was the son of Robert Stafford of Huntingdon, Gent. He was born on 17 December 1763 and matriculated at Pembroke College, Oxford in 1781, aged 17. He graduated Bachelor of Civil Law in 1788.[220] He was ordained deacon on 11 June 1786, licensed as curate to Leighton Bromswold on 12 June 1786, with a stipend of £30 p.a. and ordained Priest on 21 September 1788. He was rector of Upton and Copmanford (1789–1797). He was inducted as rector of Hemingford Abbots on 19 November 1793.[221] The living was worth approx. £300 [approx. £44,476 in 2020].[222] A tablet in the chancel records that he died, aged 32, on 29 April 1797, eight months after his wife Elizabeth, who died, aged 30, on 19 May 1796. The Parish Register records the baptisms of two children: Robert, born 8 May 1794, baptized 5 November; and William, baptized 12 January 1797.

---

[219] CCEd; https://venn.lib.cam.ac.uk/.

[220] Joseph Foster, *Alumni Oxonienses: The Members of the University of Oxford, 1715-1886: Their Parentage, Birthplace, and Year of Birth, with a Record of Their Degrees. Being the Matriculation Register of the University, Alphabetically Arranged, Revised and Annotated* (Oxford and London: Parker and co., 1887), p. 1339. https://catalog.hathitrust.org/Record/100493522.

[221] Hunts Archives Bishop's Reg XXXIX p. 580 sub book XI f.67R. The Parish Burial Register mentions that he was also Rector of Upton. CCEd.

[222] CCEd.

Figure 30 Memorial to Thomas Stafford

Charles Greene, Rector (1797–1803)

Patrons: Rogers Parker and Stanhope Pedley,
Trustees under the Will of Sir Robert Bernard, 5th Baronet

Charles Greene was born, c. 1746 in Hemingford Grey, the eldest son of Charles Greene. He was educated at Benet [Corpus Christi] College, Cambridge, a Scholar in 1764, matriculated 1765. He received his BA in 1768 and MA in 1771. He was a fellow, 1771–73.[223] Charles Greene owned Offord Darcy Manor.[224] He was the husband of Anne, daughter of Francis Blundell, who had inherited the estate from his Nailour ancestors.

---

[223] CCEd; https://venn.lib.cam.ac.uk/.

[224] Greene was the father of Charlotte Matilda, whose guardian, the Hon. Charlotte Montagu, another daughter of Francis Blundell, was lady of Offord Darcy Manor in 1806. Charlotte Matilda Greene married George Thornhill of Diddington Hall in 1809. He presented in 1814 and died in 1852. Their descendants were still at Diddington Hall until it was requisitioned in the Second World War and later demolished.

Richard Nailour had purchased the estate in 1606 and built the Manor House soon afterwards. He died in 1616.[225]

He was ordained deacon on 21 September 1771 and priest on the next day. The Presentation Deed of the Rectory of Hemingford Abbots is dated 11 April 1797,[226] and Charles Greene was instituted as Rector on 22 June. He held the following appointments: Vicar of Kimpton (1771–1773); Prebendary of Heytesbury, Horningham and Tytherington prebend, second moiety (1773–1803); Master of St John the Baptist Hospital, Wilton, (1773–1803); Prebendary of Salisbury Cathedral, where his brother Thomas was Dean, prebend of Gillingham Minor (1773–1803); Rector of Hemingford Abbots (1797–1803). He died on 20 August 1803 and was buried at Hemingford Grey.[227] His will is preserved in the Prerogative Court of Canterbury.[228]

John Pery, Rector (1803–11)

Patron: Robert Bernard Sparrow

John Pery [variant: Perry] was born, c. 1740 in Kent. He matriculated at Christchurch, Oxford on 24 May 1758, aged 18 and graduated BA in 1762, MA in 1765. He became a student[229] of Christchurch. He was ordained deacon on 22 December and priest on 14 June 1767. He married Theodosia Halsey in 1793.

He was rector of Ash, Kent (1768–78); domestic chaplain to Elizabeth Sackville, Duchess of Dorset (d. 1768) in 1767; domestic chaplain to John Frederick Sackville, 3rd Duke of Dorset (1745–99) from 1769 to 1803; preacher throughout the diocese of Lincoln (1777); rector of Houghton-cum-Wyton (1777–1811); domestic chaplain to George John Frederick Sackville, 4th Duke of Dorset, Earl of Middlesex (1793–1815) in 1803. He became rector of Hemingford Abbots on 1 October 1803.

---

[225] The changes to Offord Darcy Manor House in the late 17th and 18th centuries are described in 'The Monuments of Huntingdonshire', RCHM 1926, p. 190.

[226] Lincoln Archives DIOC/PD/153/37.

[227] Huntingdon Record Office PR Hemingford Grey: D1/2/29 fo.39.).

[228] England & Wales, Prerogative Court of Canterbury Wills, 1384–1858, PROB 11: Will Registers' 1802–1804, Piece 1397: Marriott, Quire Numbers 672–724 (1803), https://discovery.nationalarchives.gov.uk/details/r/D389477

[229] A student of Christchurch is the equivalent of a fellow at other colleges.

The Presentation Deed of the Rectory in Hemingford Abbots dates from 1803,[230] but in 1805, the house was considered unfit for residence, and it was noted that Pery 'resides upon his living of Houghton'[231] and that 'Curate Mr Banks also Vicar of the other Hemingford 1810 £50 p.a.'[232]

In 1806, the Inclosure Award consolidated land holdings in the parish.[233] The Rector benefited by being granted land adjacent to the Rectory in lieu of tithes: one fifth of open field arable land and one ninth of land subject to tithes. He was also 'exonerated and exempt from providing and keeping a bull and a boar for the use of the inhabitants of Hemingford Abbots'. 'In 1811 it was estimated that Hemingford Abbots had 1500 acres of arable, 400 of pasture, 100 of meadow, and no figures for commons, heath, fen, waste or wood.' [234]

He died at Wyton on 15 April 1811.[235] His will is preserved in the Prerogative Court of Canterbury.[236] The Rectory was in such disrepair that it was difficult to attract an incumbent.

[230] Presentation Deed 17 August 1803. Lincoln Archives DIOC/PD/159/23

[231] Survey of 1805 made in accordance with the Act of 1804 relating to residence, p. 123. Court Papers Benefice box 56/6 Lincoln Archives.

[232] *Lincoln Visitation Book* 1802–12, Vj39, p. 176. Joseph Staines Banks: https://theclergydatabase.org.uk/jsp/persons/DisplayPerson.jsp?PersonID=5604.

[233] The Inclosure Document and map are held at the Huntingdon Record Office. HP40/3/7 and CCS 35.

[234] Richard Parkinson and Board of Agriculture (Great Britain), *General View of the Agriculture of the County of Huntingdon* (London: Printed for Sherwood, Neely, and Jones, 1813) http://books.google.com/books?id=fhNLAAAAYAAJ [accessed 17 February 2022].

[235] CCEd; *Alumni Oxonienses*, 1715–1886, p. 1101.

[236] Prerogative Court of Canterbury Wills, 1384–1858 for John Pery, PROB 11: Will Registers, 1811–1814, Piece 1524: Crickett, Quire Numbers 316–68 (1811).

Archibald Eyre Obins, Rector (1811–38)

Patron: Lady Olivia Bernard Sparrow

A change of patron brought a different kind of clergyman. Lady Olivia Bernard Sparrow[237] appointed her cousin Archibald Eyre Obins. Both were grandchildren of Sir Archibald Acheson, 1st Viscount Gosford.[238] Archibald Eyre Obins (1776–1868) was educated at the Armagh Royal School before entering Trinity College, Dublin. His family came from Castle Obins in Armagh. Archibald was the last to live there, but the property was sold in 1820 to Robert Bernard Sparrow, the husband of Lady Olivia.

The County Armagh Yeomanry was formed in 1796–9, and he is recorded as Commanding Officer of the Portadown Cavalry, with the rank of Captain.[239] He matriculated at Exeter College, Oxford in 1797 and graduated BA in 1799, MA in 1811. From 1805–07, he was Private

---

[237] See above, pp. 25f.

[238] Archibald Obins (b. 1773 in Portadown, County Armagh) was the son of Michael Obins (d. 1798) and Nicola Acheson (1728–1821).

[239] The events that led up to the formation of the Yeomanry Corps in Ireland in 1796 had their roots in the French Revolution in 1789. Parliamentary independence had been granted to the Irish Parliament in 1782. The suppression of protest groups led to subversive elements becoming better organized. The government reacted with an Insurrection Act in 1793 and then encouraged the formation of Yeomanry Corps. The War Office in Dublin Castle granted authority to prominent members of the gentry in Armagh to form between eighteen and twenty-two cavalry and infantry corps under named Commanding Officers, one of whom was Obins. The anticipated rebellion broke out in 1798, when Obins was at Oxford, and was suppressed, more by the Yeomanry than by the weak and scattered regular forces. S. C. Lutton, 'County Armagh Yeomanry', *Journal of Craigavon Historical Society*, vol. 1, no. 2 (1970), https://www.craigavonhistoricalsociety.org.uk/rev/luttonyeomanry.php.

Secretary to Lord William Bentinck, Governor of Madras.[240] Obins, like most of his family, was a freemason.[241]

He became Rector of Hemingford Abbots, near his cousin Lady Olivia Sparrow's estate in Huntingdonshire, from 1811. The presentation deed of 1811 for Hemingford Abbots records: '1811 April 15. Rector of Hemingford Abbots. Patron, Lady Olivia Bernard Sparrow of Brampton Park, widow.'[242] Major alterations were made to the rectory house during the next four years. The present frontage was added, ceilings were raised, and the coach-house was built.

[240] Lord William Bentinck was appointed Governor of Madras in 1803 and was promoted from colonel to major-general in 1805. Although his tenure as Governor was moderately successful, it was brought to an end by a mutiny at Vellore in 1806, prompted by Bentinck's order that the native troops be forbidden to wear their traditional attire. Only after serious violence was order restored and the offending policy rescinded, and Bentinck was recalled in 1807. He returned to India as the first Governor-General of India from 1828 to 1835. Bentinck married Mary, daughter of Arthur Acheson, 1st Earl of Gosford, on 18 February 1803. He died in Paris on 17 June 1839, aged 64. Mary died in May 1843. Mary's elder sister Olivia had married on 14 March 1797 Brigadier-General Robert Bernard Sparrow of Brampton Park, Huntingdon, and Tanderagee Castle, Armagh, who died of fever in the West Indies aged 32 in 1805. She was Patron of Hemingford Abbots for the 58 years of her widowhood and died in 1863. Olivia and Mary's brother, Archibald the 2nd Earl, had married Mary Sparrow of Worlingham Hall, Suffolk, in the previous month in 1805. The father of Archibald, Olivia and Mary had a sister Nicola, who married Michael Obins of Castle Obins, Armagh. She died in 1821 while Archibald Obins was Rector at Hemingford Abbots and Olivia Sparrow was Patron. There is a monument to Nicola Obins on the south wall of the chancel.

[241] See *Portadown Times*, 12 February 1954, p. 4.

[242] Hunts Archives AH26/237/90. Rectory Presentation Deed 11 April 1811 Lincoln Archives DIOC/PD/167/27.

Figure 31 Memorial to Nichola Obins, mother of Archibald

In 1813, Obins was granted a licence for non-residence,[243] and in 1817 a curate, John Buddell, was receiving a stipend.[244] On 28 September 1818, there was a statement of 'actual inability to the Duties of your own or any other cure'.[245] Further stipendiary curates were appointed: in 1818, Morgan Davies; 1821, Charles Martin Torlesse; 1823, Benjamin George Blackden; 1825, Ralph Wilde; and 1834, Henry Lewis Davies. Their stipends were between £100 and £120. In 1818 it was added that the stipend was 'with surplice, fees and the use of house during the absence of the Rector, and on his return suitable accommodation in the parish at the Rector's expense.' Despite the evangelical leanings of the rector, the use of the surplice indicates broad-church tendencies, indeed the surplice was seen as a badge of Popery by some in the Church of England.[246]

---

[243] Licence for non-residence, Hunts Archives AH27/1/271/123.

[244] Curate stipend Hunts Archives AH27/1/271/148. CCEd.

[245] Inability. Hunts Archives AH27/1/271/158, Archibald Eyre Obins, Hemingford Abbots. 'On account of actual inability to the Duties of your own or any other cure.' 28 Sept 1818'. https://discovery.nationalarchives.gov.uk/details/r/e3217a64-e74e-4c4b-8065-61ca10caec25.

[246] Cf. David Yeandle, *A Victorian Curate: A Study of the Life and Career of the Rev. Dr John Hunt* (Cambridge, UK: Open Book Publishers, 2021) https://doi.org/10.11647/OBP.0248, p. 73.

Figure 32 Royal Coat of Arms, St Margaret's, 1814

In 1814, the Royal Coat of Arms was installed in the church.[247] In the following year, the terms of the Congress of Vienna elevated Hanover to be an independent kingdom under George III of Great Britain. The helm

[247] The 'Achievement of Arms' is situated in the south aisle, west of the doorway, but previously was probably hung on a tympanum high in the chancel arch. It was restored by Justin Hawkes in 2018. Some churches with royal patronage had displayed the royal arms since the reign of Henry III (1216–1272). Others later displayed them to show loyalty to Henry VIII rather than the Pope, after the break from Rome. At the restoration of the monarchy in 1660 Parliament ordained that the Royal Arms should be set up in churches, but this was not compulsory. In the 18th century most, English churches displayed them; about 20% still do so.

in the Royal Arms was then replaced by a crown. It is probable that the Coat of Arms in St Margaret's was sponsored by the patron, Lady Olivia Bernard Sparrow, who had been widowed nine years earlier.

In June 1822, Obins accompanied Lady and Miss Sparrow in the 'steam packet' boat from Dover to Boulogne-sur-Mer. His curate, Charles Torlesse (1795–1881), substituted for him at Hemingford Abbots, and a terrier of the glebe land was carried out. An interesting correspondence between Torlesse and Obins and tributes to Torlesse survives between Obins in Boulogne and Torlesse in Hemingford Abbots rectory.[248] Torlesse took a particular interest in the quality of the singing.[249] There is also evidence that Lady Olivia Sparrow continued to exercise her influence and that the incumbent must comply with her wishes. After a couple of years, Torlesse was inducted as vicar of Stoke-by-Nayland, Suffolk, where he served for 58 years. He included Obins as a second name for his son Charles. It was in 1826, three years after Torlesse left Hemingford Abbots, that a small, movable organ was placed in a gallery at the west end. The galleries were extended in 1868 for school children.

The sterling silver Communion set, donated at this time, is still used on special occasions. Each piece is inscribed 'Hemingford Abbots Church 1826', and a round cartouche on each has a sunburst motif. Their markings show that the pair of chalices and flagon were made in 1795–96 by John Rowe, and the paten in 1800–01 by Stephen Adams. The salver with the same cartouche was made in 1719 by William Gamble.

---

[248] http://www.thekingscandlesticks.com/webs/pedigrees/2/32701.html.

[249] 'I was pleased to observe the grateful mention [Wm. John] made of your name, and the sense he expressed of your great attention to him. He also spoke much of your exertions in the parish. I had not previously heard of the pains you were taking with the singers. This must be very grateful to the people and is very acceptable to me. I am very anxious to have good singing, and as I believe I told you to have the singing [in] general, that everyone who can join may join. This and the repeating the responses aloud, adds considerably to the effect of our service, and gives an animation very [much] wanting where this is not practised. It is according to the Rubric, it also makes the people use their prayer books, we must work for this when we meet.' (ibid.).

Figure 33 Silver paten, 1826

Repairs to the church during Obins's incumbency included the steeple in 1822, the raising of the chancel walls and a new east window in 1826, the re-leading and glazing of the windows in 1828 and the clock in 1835.

In 1832, Obins officiated at a wedding of another relative of the Obins and Acheson families.[250] He retired from Hemingford Abbots in 1838.

Obins was evidently an inspiring, moderately evangelical preacher, and for this, he drew the admiration of Potto Brown, who notes how 'In Houghton and the villages grouped around, as well as in St. Ives, there appears to have been a dearth of spiritual life', indeed he refers to them as 'strongholds of sin', and he praises Selwyn, Obins's successor, for his evangelical preaching, noting that Obins's 'gospel ministry attracted so many hearers from the parishes round', while the 'congregational churches at St. Ives were formal and cold; the Quakers impassive; the

[250] '1832—Marriage ceremony conducted by the Rev. Archibald Eyre Obins; Edmund Bacon, Esq., eldest son of Sir Edmund Bacon of Raveningham Hall, Norfolk, married Louisa, 3rd dau of the late William Richardson, Esq. of Rich Hill, Co. Armagh [note that Richardson family related to Acheson family].' https://www.genealogy.com/forum/surnames/topics/acheson/624/.

Methodist community was the most missionary …'[251] However, as re-
gards alms-giving, Obins comes in for censure, this time from Bateman
Brown:

> I remember also that a former Rector of Hemingford Abbots, the
> Rev. Mr. Obins, committed the same error (he was the Rev.
> Selwyn's immediate predecessor). By indiscriminate alms-giv-
> ing, he made Hemingford one of the worst villages in the neigh-
> bourhood. My father knew him well, as also did I. He had a cu-
> rate a very popular preacher, whom, when my father first left
> the Society of Friends, he often used to go and hear. His name
> was Keyle, and he published a volume of sermons which I now
> have.[252]

Brown goes on to provide an interesting snippet regarding Obins, which
points to some disquiet in the parish and may explain why Obins was
granted a licence for non-residence in 1813.

> To return to Mr. Obins. He resigned his living in disgust, and
> some years afterwards was returning from Huntingdon to Lon-
> don, after a visit to Lady Sparrow, when my father, on getting
> into the railway carriage, and finding a gentleman he knew, be-
> gan to talk to him. The subject of indiscriminate alms-giving
> came up, my father quoting Mr. Obins as an example. The gen-
> tleman: This is Mr. Obins sitting by the side of you. Not having
> seen him for many years, my father had quite forgotten him, and
> began to apologise. Mr. Obins replied, "No apology is necessary;
> no one is more conscious of the harm I did than myself."[253]

In the 1851 Census for Birkenhead, we find Obins living at 65 Parkfield,
aged 77:

[251] Neville Goodman, C. P. Tebbutt, R. W. Dixon, and H. Allon, *Potto Brown: The
Village Philanthropist* [Four Essays] (St Ives: A. Goodman, 1878)
https://books.google.co.uk/books?id=_9H2VLU8R6oC, p. 121.
[252] Bateman Brown, *Reminiscences of Bateman Brown, J.P.* (Peterborough: Peterborough Advertiser Co., 1905), pp. 135f. Keyle may refer to Robert Wood Kyle,
CCEd Person ID: 14761.
[253] *Ibid.*, p. 136.

Unmarried. Head of Household. Occupation 'Clergyman not having cure of souls' Also at the address: Elizabeth Leaver 44 Housekeeper unmarried, b. Berkshire; Ann Taylor 19 Housemaid unmarried b. Cheshire?; George Anderson 29 House servant unmarried b. Durham

In the 1861 Census for Walcot, Somerset, entry 71, Obins is again recorded, living at 21 St James Square Age 87:

Unmarried. Head of Household. Occupation 'Rector without cure of souls'. Also at the address: Edward Fry, 37, Butler unmarried b. Hampshire; Harriet Burch, 50, Domestic servant unmarried b. Surrey; Margaret Brown, 33, Housemaid unmarried b. Cumberland.[254]

He died on 6 January 1868 at Bath, aged 95. His residence was in 21 St James's Square, Bath. Probate was on 29 January in Bristol. He left effects under £14,000 [£1,618,960 in 2020]. Burial was on 11 January at Bath Abbey (St Peter & St Paul).

John Buddell, Stipendiary Curate (1817)

John Buddell was born on 10 April 1789 in Little Walsingham, Norfolk. He was a sizar at Corpus Christi College, Cambridge in 1807, afterwards a scholar. He took his BA in 1812 and his MA in 1820. He was ordained deacon on 21 June 1812 and priest on 29 December 1813. He was about 27 when at Hemingford Abbots. He appears never to have held his own living. He held the following appointments: Curate of West Tofts (1812); Mundford (1812); Willersey (1820); Stipendiary Curate of Willersey (1820); Hinton on the Green (1820); Marston Sicca (1823); Stibbard (1828). He died on 23 January 1858 in Marychurch, Torquay, Devon.

[254] There had been a possible previous Obins family connection with Walcot in 1805, when Joseph Stock, who was Lord Bishop of Killala from 1798 to 1810, married secondly a widow Mary Ann Obins, née Thomas, of Walcot, near Bath. He died on 13 August 1813.

Morgan Davies, Stipendiary Curate (1818)

Morgan Davies was licensed as stipendiary curate on 7 October 1818. His stipend was '£105 [approx. £9,199 in 2020] with surplice fees and use of a house during the absence of the Rector, and on his return suitable accommodation in the parish at the Rector's expense.' He was a BA of Jesus College, Oxford, where he matriculated on 20 June 1815, aged 22, and received his BA in 1820.[255] He was ordained deacon on 21 September 1817. He held the following appointments: stipendiary curate of Brampton (1817), of Hemingford Abbots (1818), and curate of Astley (1820).[256]

Reign of George IV (1820–1830)

Charles Martin Torlesse, Stipendiary Curate (1821–23)

Figure 34 Charles Martin Torlesse

Charles Torlesse was born on 29 May 1795 in Bloomsbury. He was educated at Harrow School and Trinity College, Cambridge, where he

---

[255] *Alumni Oxonienses*, 1715–1886, p. 349.

[256] CCEd 6699.

matriculated in 1814, graduating BA in 1818 and MA in 1821. He was ordained deacon in 1821 and priest in 1822. He was licensed to Hemingford Abbots on 17 June 1821, aged 26.[257] He served as Curate of Stoke-by-Nayland, Suffolk, from 1824 and Vicar from 1832 to 1881. He died, aged 86, on 12 July 1881.[258]

Benjamin George Blackden, Stipendiary Curate (1823)

Benjamin Blackden was licensed as stipendiary curate on 30 October 1823. His stipend was £105 [approx. £9,199 in 2020]. He was born, c. 1792 in Cannock, Staffordshire. He was a pensioner at St John's College, Cambridge (1809) and migrated to Queens', from whence he received his BA in 1814 and MA in 1818. He was admitted to Lincoln's Inn in 1813, ordained deacon on 11 June 1815 and priest on 20 December 1818. Appointments held were: Stipendiary Curate, Great Tey (1815); curate, Shirburn (1818); curate, Pyrton (1818); stipendiary curate, Hemingford Abbots (1823); rector, Thorpe, Derbyshire (1824).[259] He died on 10 April 1852, aged 60.

Ralph Wilde, Stipendiary Curate (1825)

Ralph Wilde was born in Dublin on 9 August 1798, the eldest brother of the well-known surgeon and antiquarian William Wilde, who was the father of the playwright Oscar.[260] After obtaining his BA in 1824 at Trinity College Dublin, he was ordained deacon on 13 June 1824 and priest on 29 May 1825. The CCEd records that he held five stipendiary curacies at Pakefield, near Lowestoft, Suffolk (1824); Hemingford Abbots (1825); Atherstone, Warwickshire (1830); Kingswood (Bitton) near Bristol (1831); and Carisbrooke, Newport Chapel (Isle of Wight) (1834).

The 1861 Census sees him in Staffordshire as the perpetual curate of Upper Gornal, a widower together with Emily 13 and Mary 11, who were Oscar Wilde's half-sisters, having been born out of wedlock before

---

[257] CCEd. On his time at Hemingford Abbots, see above, pp. 85f.

[258] For a full biography, see *The Kings Candlesticks*: http://www.thekingscandlesticks.com/webs/pedigrees/1633.html.

[259] CCEd; https://venn.lib.cam.ac.uk/.

[260] https://www.irishtimes.com/news/the-surgical-intellect-of-the-senior-wilde-1.308828.

their father's marriage, and were wards of their uncle Ralph. Their father was Sir William Wilde (1815–76), an eminent surgeon.[261] By the time of the 1871 census, he was the perpetual curate of Bretherton, still living together with his nieces. A rare character sketch of the man in 1871 exists, which, while no doubt not describing his more youthful characteristics during his time in Hemingford Abbots, nevertheless offers insights into the personality of the curate:

> The clergyman to whom we are alluding is the Rev. Ralph Wilde. He is a diminutive, grey-headed man—sharp in look, active in gait, a wearer of spectacles, and venerable. He is upwards of 70 years old, and has fair wear in him yet. Mr. Wilde has Hibernian blood in his veins; but he is not an absolutely '*wild*' Irishman, for in his pedigree there is a mixture of Anglo Saxon metal, which gives the necessary compensating power. He took his degree of B.A. at Dublin, in 1824; was, in the first instance, curate of Lowestoft; then curate of Birmingham, under Dr. Marsh; was afterwards curate at Tarleton church, under the late Rev. Streynsham Master; held this position for eight years then took a curacy near Bilston, in Staffordshire; and came to Bretherton early in 1862. His salary is only £136 per annum. Mr Wilde is a pretty good reader but not such a wonderful preacher, is active in habit, slightly impulsive, has no faith in £136 a year—particularly when he can see how other gentlemen of his cloth in the district are paid; can't make headway in Bretherton, owing to either personal inability or the obtusity of the natives; doesn't seem to sail along the stream of time very complacently in the district—is unable to get the people of Bretherton into a state of ecstacy [sic] concerning the Rev. Ralph Wilde and can't break down the strong Dissenting spirit which exists in the locality.[262]

[261] *Ibid*.

[262] *Preston Chronicle*, 15 April 1871, p. 6. Apart from his first curacy near Lowestoft, this press report indicates that after the Isle of Wight he probably moved to Birmingham, though this may refer to Upper Gornal in the 1861 census, which

Wilde moved in 1871 to North Monaghan in Ireland. In November 1871, both his nieces, aged 24 and 22, died after their crinoline dresses had caught fire at a Hallowe'en ball in Drumaconnor House, Co. Monaghan, the home of a Mr Reid. Ralph Wilde lived for another eleven years and died in 1882.[263]

Reign of William IV (1830–37)

Henry Lewis Davies, Stipendiary Curate (1834)

Henry Davies was born at Llandysiliogogo, Cardiganshire, Wales, c. 1800. He was licensed at Hemingford Abbots as stipendiary curate on 4 July 1834. He had been ordained deacon on 12 October 1823 and priest on 17 October 1824. He held the following appointments: stipendiary curate, Llandysiliogogo with Llangrannog (1823); curate, Papworth St Agnes (1828); stipendiary curate, Hemingford Abbots (1834). It is noted in the Lincoln Curates Register of Licences (1831–40) that his stipend would be £120 [approx. £15,950 in 2020] and that he would reside in the parish.[264] He was Vicar of Kenarth, Newcastle Emlyn, Cardiganshire, from 1852. Its population was 404, about 15% smaller than Hemingford Abbots. His income was £210, with a vicarage and 4 acres of glebe land, and the 1871 census recorded that he was still living there at that date. He died, aged 81, in 1881.

is in the west Midlands. He then moved to Tarleton in Lancashire before returning to Bilston, only 5 miles from Upper Gornal. Eight years later he returned to Lancashire, Bretherton being only 3 miles from Tarleton.

263 Cf. Michelle McGoff-McCann, *Melancholy Madness: A Coroner's Casebook* (Cork: Mercier, 2003); http://www.irishidentity.com/extras/gaels/stories/wilde.htm.

264 CCEd 6699.

Reign of Victoria (1837–1901)

Edward Selwyn, Rector (1838–67)

Patron: Lady Olivia Bernard Sparrow

Figure 35 Edward Selwyn

Edward Selwyn was born in Gloucester in 1793, the youngest son of Captain Henry Charles Selwyn (1751–1807) and Sarah Thomson (1760–1820).[265] They were married in Quebec, Canada on 8 June 1775. Capt. Selwyn was Lt. Gov. of Montserrat and head of the Selwyns of Matson House, Gloucestershire, although the estate had by then passed down the female line to Viscount Sydney. Edward Selwyn was educated at the Royal Military Academy, Woolwich, having been sponsored by Lord Sydney's sister, Mary Townshend, and commissioned into the Royal Artillery (Lieutenant, served in the War against America of 1812).

---

[265] https://www.geni.com/people/Rev-Edward-Selwyn/6000000069525901067.

He matriculated in 1820 and was ordained after graduating BA in 1824 from St Catherine's College, Cambridge.[266] He served for 15 years as Vicar of Ruddington, Nottinghamshire. (1823–38), including the last five years also as priest in charge of Edwalton.

Edward Selwyn was married first in Bromley on 2 Sep 1818 to Frances (Fanny) (1791–1848), daughter of the Rev. John Simons of St Paul's Cray, Kent (Patron: Lord Sydney), a well-known evangelical preacher, and his wife, daughter of William Sturges of Datchet and Bradford, partner in the Bowling Iron Works. Edward was a shareholder and partner, too, and served as Curate of St Paul's Cray in 1823.

They had six children: (1) Maria Elizabeth Selwyn (1820–93); (2) Rev Edward John Selwyn (1822–93), Headmaster of Blackheath School, who was in turn father of Edward Carus, Headmaster of Uppingham, in turn father of Edward Gordon, Dean of Winchester in the mid-twentieth century; (3) Frederick Michael Selwyn (1825–59); (4) William Marshall Selwyn (1825–68) of Longwood Hall, Bingley, also an Ironmaster and great-great-grandfather of a current contact Richard Selwyn Sharpe QC, of Yorkshire; (5) Fanny Mary Anne Selwyn (1827–96) and (6) Matilda Charlotte Selwyn (1833–82).

He was inducted as Rector of Hemingford Abbots in 1838 and soon commanded respect in the area. For example, he was involved in the opening of the schools at Hemingford Abbots in 1840 and Swavesey in 1841.[267] The attractiveness of Selwyn's sermons to liberal dissenters in the area was mentioned by Bateman Brown, son of Houghton's miller Potto Brown.[268]

---

[266] https://venn.lib.cam.ac.uk/.

[267] *Cambridge Chronicle and Journal*, Saturday, 25 September 1841 p. 2.

[268] Cf. Bateman Brown, *Reminiscences*, pp. 51f.: 'It is perfectly true that a great many workpeople and others, besides those connected with my father, forsook their Parish Church because of the inefficiency of the Rector, as described previously, and went over to the Parish Church of Hemingford Abbots, where there was a very energetic, good, Christian man, who was also a very popular preacher, viz., the Rev. Mr. Selwin. Frequently there would be a company of 100 seen crossing the meadow to go to Hemingford Church, because they could get no spiritual benefit at their own Parish Church. I may say here in passing, that Mr. Goodman and my father, prior to the time I am recording, would frequently

After ten years in Hemingford Abbots, Fanny died on 26 August 1848.[269] In April 1849, Selwyn was granted a licence for non-residence owing to 'the unfitness of Glebe House and ill-health of your family'. In 1850, Edward Selwyn married secondly Fanny Margetts (1806–91), who had been born in Hemingford Grey. The 1851 Census recorded that he and Fanny were living at the Rector's House with a house servant and cook.

In 1851, there was a national Census of Religious Worship. Clemmow noted that Hemingford Abbots had shifted, since 1676, from having one of the highest levels of dissent in Huntingdonshire to having one of the highest indexes of Anglican attendance in 1851.[270] He identified several factors in this change. The Church of England had become more inclusive, especially in parishes such as Hemingford Abbots where Selwyn was the only evangelical clergyman in the immediate area. The proportion of the population attending morning service was among the highest in the county at 43% (232 of 544). Second, the rise in the number of Quakers had been at the expense of the Baptists and, thirdly, increasing prosperity and literacy had been reflected in a 'waning appetite for dissent'.[271]

In 1860, aged 67, Selwyn, together with many conservative clergy, including Yate Fosbroke and his successor as Vicar of St Ives, Charles D. Goldie, signed a petition against the controversial progressive liberal publication *Essays and Reviews*. Frederick S. Ramsden of Hemingford Abbots was also a signatory.[272]

---

go to hear Mr. Selwin, accompanied by their families, because no spiritual good was to be obtained from the Nonconformist Minister at St. Ives.'

[269] Selwyn wrote a touching tribute to his wife upon her death in a Bible, reproduced in manuscript: https://selwyn-family.me.uk/genealogy/showmedia.php?mediaID=6&medialinkID=6&tngpage=1.

[270] Clemmow, p. 205.

[271] 'A superior socio-economic profile indicative of a higher level of literacy, and effective pastoral care, appear to have contributed to a 'conversion' to conformity.' Clemmow, p. 208.

[272] *To the Most Reverend Father in God, John Bird, Lord Archbishop of Canterbury ... We the Undersigned, Clergy of the United Church of England and Ireland, Etc. [An Address Directed against Certain Opinions Contained in "Essays and Reviews"]*, 1860 https://books.google.co.uk/books?id=Qu2-Z1uss0EC, p. 29.

Edward Selwyn is mentioned in a book about the Hart family, as Thomas Hart I was Sexton and Clerk for fifty years until his death in 1866, when his son Thomas was appointed by Selwyn to succeed his father as Clerk.[273] Thomas II also served as Parish Constable. His occupation was thatcher and cordwainer, or shoemaker. James, a younger son of Thomas Hart II, reacted in his teens and became a Baptist. Selwyn tried hard to dissuade him. Later, in 1847, James Hart joined the Mormons and was one of the early wagon train settlers in Salt Lake City and Idaho. Some of his descendants still visit the village from the USA.

Selwyn died on 14 September 1867. He is buried in the churchyard on the south side of the west end of St Margaret's Church.

Figure 36 Edward Selwyn's tombstone

There were 541 people living in the parish at the census in 1841. It did not reach this size again until the 1950s. At the last census, in 2011, the population was 635.

[273] Edward LeRoy Hart, *Mormon in Motion: The Life and Journals of James H. Hart, 1825–1906, in England, France, and America* (Utah: Windsor Books, 1978), pp 4f. and 1851 Census & Vestry Book for 1866. Thomas I, a Master Thatcher, had married Elizabeth Marriott, whose family lived where Barn Hall was built in 1869. Manorial Records show that he was paid for capping a barn in 1859.

Several present homes in the village were built during the 29 years of early Victorian England while Edward Selwyn served here. These included Hemingford Park and the terraced north side of the High Street. The school for 70 children was open from 1840 to 1978,[274] and the railway from Godmanchester to St Ives passed through the parish from 1847 to 1960. The Wellingtonia tree in the Rectory garden was planted in 1852 to commemorate the death of the Duke of Wellington.

However, the industrial revolution and the drift to the towns resulted in the number of families declining by over a third between 1851 and 1891. Notably, the number of farmworkers halved from 142 to 72. As with many rural parishes at the time, Selwyn's successor, Henry Herbert, faced the challenges of a parish that was changing and contracting significantly.

Henry Herbert, Rector (1867–1911)

Patron: Dennis Herbert

Figure 37 Henry Herbert

[274] Cf. David Yeandle, 'Hemingford Abbots' School' http://www.hemlocs.co.uk /Abbotsschool.html.

Figure 38 Mary Herbert in middle age

Henry Herbert was born in Huntingdon in 1824. He was educated at Eton, where his mother's brother, Richard Okes, was Lower Master. After three years at Worcester College Oxford, he went to Cape Town and taught at the school founded by his mother's uncle, the Rev. Holt Okes. Three years later, in 1848, Bishop Gray arrived as the first English Bishop of South Africa.[275] His brother lived in Godmanchester, and it is likely that the Gray and Herbert families knew each other. When Bishop Gray opened a new school at Protea, which still flourishes as Bishop's College, Rondebosch, he appointed Henry Herbert as the assistant master. Henry's character and cricketing abilities made him a much-valued asset. Bishop Gray trained Henry for Holy Orders, ordaining him Deacon in 1849 and priest in 1855. After 11 years in South Africa, Henry returned in the following year to England where he held curacies in Suffolk and Buckinghamshire.

The sale of the family's Brewery and public houses in Huntingdon in 1864 by Dennis Herbert facilitated significant changes in Henry's life as an impoverished curate. Dennis bought the advowson of Hemingford

[275] Cf. https://en.wikipedia.org/wiki/Robert_Gray_(bishop_of_Cape_Town).

Abbots and presented his half-brother Henry as Rector in 1868. At the age of 43, Henry was at last able to afford to marry Mary Ruddock. This took place five days after his induction as Rector. They had six sons over the next decade.

Figure 39 Mary Herbert in youth

Henry was inducted as Rector in January 1868 and also served as Rural Dean of Huntingdon from 1874 to 1894. The agricultural depression of the 1870s and 1880s hit clergy incomes hard. Despite Henry's own difficulties he had to console many other country parsons as well as his own parishioners.

In a letter (8 January 1888) in response to questioning in relation to seeking aid for support for university fees he stated 'The income of this Living is derived from Glebe Farm which, after being on my hands some time was let from last Michaelmas at 9/- per acre instead of 28/- and 30/- as in previous years (430 acres). I have six boys to provide for and my private income does not amount to £200 (£26,583 in 2020) and am therefore obliged to draw from capital.'

Figure 40 The Herbert family, early 20th century

Henry and Mary were caring and active in the parish. Their support for the school is one example. Their daughter-in-law Madeline, Francis's widow, wrote in 1978, when the school closed 'Before the Education Act in 1902 when all schools were taken over by the State I think the Revd HH paid for everything …they used to pay 2d per child per week if they could afford it … at one time they had a school mistress and gave her a room at the Rectory, gave her food and no doubt paid her salary!'

The village contracted by a third between 1851 and 1891, when there were only 354 residents. Although the number of farmers and farm-workers halved over the same period, there were still ten families employing resident servants in 1891.

Nevertheless, there were several major building projects on the church during the 1870s, including repairs to both aisles, the clerestories, the chancel, and the south porch. The Resurrection window in the south aisle by Clayton & Bell dates from 1875 and the depiction of Jesus with children by Heaton, Butler & Bayne from 1873.[276] The tower was restored in 1887. The organ, replacing an earlier movable instrument, was installed in 1906.[277]

Figure 41 St Margaret's church interior before 1906

[276] Jesus and children, Day, pp. 12, 22, 26, 64 (See Figure 58 Sholto-Douglas window, p. 126, below). Resurrection window, Day, pp. 22, 88 (See Figure 54 The Linton window, p. 117, below).

[277] https://www.npor.org.uk/NPORView.html?RI=N03101.

Figure 42 The organ in 2021

Figure 43 Sketch of Henry Herbert by J. Blake Wirgman

At the turn of the century, Henry Herbert was 76. The Vicar of Hemingford Grey, Mr Curtois, had been tragically killed by a train while using a railway bridge as a short cut over the flooded meadows to Houghton.

In 1899, Hemingford Grey welcomed his successor, the 39-year-old Rev. Byrom Holland, who 'brought all parts of the Hemingford villages together through their involvement in the Regatta … He seems to have been a modest man, his quietness belying the strength of his leadership.'[278] It is a tribute to him that the Regatta continues to thrive, interrupted only occasionally by events such as the Covid pandemic in 2021.

Henry suffered a serious stroke in 1908 and was effectively disabled. His youngest son, Francis, had been ordained two years previously and was a curate in Marlow. Francis moved to Hemingford Abbots and married Madeline King in 1909. Madeline wrote (26 July 1967) 'I used to plan his tasty dishes as the nurses gave him bread and milk for each meal until he called out in revolt! … His charm and courtesy were something to remember.' Henry died on 27 July 1911. Francis was presented as Rector by his aunt Caroline, who had inherited the patronage. Henry's widow, Mary, died in 1917.

His eldest son, Dennis Henry, entered Parliament in 1918 as Conservative MP for Watford and was knighted in 1929. He served as Deputy Speaker from 1931 to 1943, when he was raised to the peerage and chose the title Baron Hemingford. His son, Dennis, the second Lord, who succeeded in 1947, purchased the Old Rectory from the Church Commissioners and served as Lord Lieutenant of the County of Huntingdon and Peterborough from 1968 to 1974. He died in 1982 and was succeeded by his son Nicholas, the present Lord Hemingford.[279]

A full account of Henry Herbert's life is contained in his great-grandson's history of the family, *Successive Journeys: A Family in Four Continents* by Nicholas Herbert, 3rd Lord Hemingford (2008).[280]

---

[278] Bridget Flanagan, *A Story of Village Rowing: Hemingfords' Regatta 1901–2001* (Hemingford Grey: Bridget Flanagan, 2001), p. 9.

[279] This paragraph is a quotation from an unpublished typescript entitled 'Hemingford Abbots' by Richard Butterfield, Pam Dearlove, Nicholas Hemingford and David Peace (c. 1997).

[280] Nicholas Herbert, *Successive Journeys: A Family in Four Continents* (Gamlingay: Authors OnLine, 2008).

Figure 44 Henry Herbert memorial window

The east window of the chancel in the church by James Powell & Sons of Whitefriars depicts the Crucifixion.[281] It was donated by the village in 1913 and is a fine memorial to Henry, who had been Rector for over forty years. The depiction of Christ's crucifixion has the inscription 'Ego sum vitis vera': ('I am the true vine'), with the cross being like a vine stem. The figures below the cross represent the Virgin Mary and St John. From the left the others are St Peter, the first apostle; St Margaret of Antioch, the patron saint of the church, with dragon; St Augustine, the first Primate of the Church in England; and above are St Benedict, the founder of the Benedictine order of Ramsey Abbey and St Patrick, the patron saint of Ireland. On the right are St Alban, martyred where St Alban's Abbey is now; St Etheldreda, bearing Ely Cathedral, which she founded; St George, the patron saint of England; and above are St Columba, who founded the Iona Community; and St Aidan of Lindisfarne. Apart from Jesus's mother Mary and his disciples John and Peter, the others died between 303 and 679 AD.

Figure 45 St Margaret's church, c. 1913–32

[281] Day, pp. 33, 50, 67.

Reign of Edward VII (1901–10)

None appointed.

Reign of George V (1910–36)

Francis Herbert, Rector (1911–25)

Patron: Caroline Herbert

Figure 46 Francis Falkner Herbert, c. 1908

Francis Herbert was the youngest of six sons of Henry Herbert, Rector of Hemingford Abbots, and his wife Mary. He was born in 1879, when his father was 55 and his mother 45, and was ten years younger than his oldest brother, Dennis. He was 'popular, handsome, charming and a good sportsman' according to his great-nephew, Nicholas Herbert. After Emmanuel College Cambridge and Wells Theological College, in 1904, he was appointed as a curate in Great Marlow. He was ordained priest in 1906 and came to Hemingford Abbots a couple of years later as curate, when his father suffered a stroke.

In 1909 Francis married Madeline King from Catworth, the daughter of a corn merchant. They lived in Thorpe Cottage at the east end of the village. Francis was appointed Rector after Henry's death in 1911 and moved into the Rectory with his wife and son.

They had been actively involved in the parish, Madeline with the Mothers' Union and both of them in the Regatta. Francis was elected its President in 1913, and Madeline presented the prizes. 'The whole day was marked by a spirit of simple enjoyment and harmony of feeling' remarked the local newspaper. Their two sons, Kenneth and Henry, were born in 1910 and 1915.

In 1915, the renovation of the east window in the chancel was completed, commemorating Henry's 44 years as Rector. Stained glass by Powell of Whitefriars was set in stonework designed by Inskip Ladds, the diocesan surveyor and architect. The Dickens family had given permission for the previous stained glass to be removed to the east end of the north aisle.

The gutters were renewed, and drains laid round the church. These and other significant building works involved the church being closed for four months. It reopened in 1915, and Francis wanted to hold a thanksgiving service, but the Bishop of Ely, Rt. Rev. Dr. Frederic Chase, considered this should be postponed until the final £80 of the cost of the works had been raised. The Bishop would be on holiday on 12th July and was not pleased to hear that not only was it going ahead but that the Archdeacon had been asked to preach: 'Thus precisely that happened which I desired to prevent.' (23rd September 1915)

After Francis's mother Mary died in 1917, he joined up as an Army Chaplain and was posted to the East Midlands. He was ill in 1919, and his income from tenant farmers declined while the expenses involved in maintaining his family and the Rectory increased.

A brass plaque in the nave records the names of the seven parishioners who were killed during the first world war, and a list of those who served in the armed forces is displayed in the north aisle. A framed 'Roll of Honour' lists all those from Hemingford Abbots who fought in the Great War.

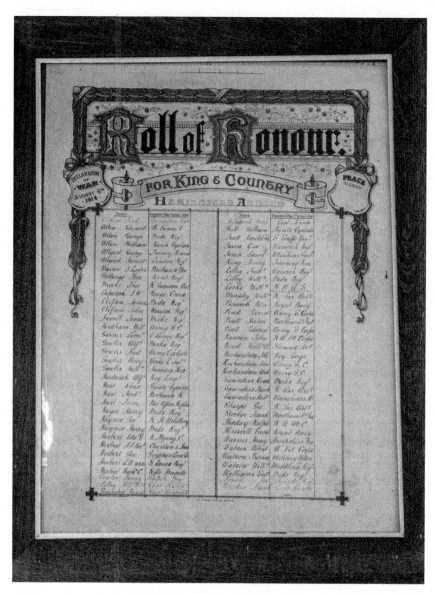

Figure 47 Roll of Honour

The first meeting of the newly introduced Parochial Church Council took place in April 1920,[282] with 194 parishioners entitled to vote. Francis was Chairman, and Churchwarden Colonel Linton was Vice-Chairman. In 1922, part of the Glebe Land known as 'Townlands' was sold, and repairs to the tower were carried out, together with repointing of the aisles. A Restoration Fund was started in 1923 with the proceeds of a tennis tournament in 1924 and a fete at Hemingford Park in 1925.

Figure 48 Francis Falkner Herbert in middle age

In 1923, the Easter offering in church was given to the rector for the first time for several years. Francis's brothers Dennis and Teddie tried to help

[282] The Minutes of Hemingford Abbots Parochial Church Council are the source of much of the detail about the parish from 1920 onwards

with his financial affairs, which had been deteriorating and were in crisis by 1924.

In that year, the recently appointed Bishop of Ely, Leonard White-Thompson, who did not know of his difficulties, appointed him to additional responsibilities as Rural Dean, with the assurance that this was essentially a pastoral role, supporting his fellow clergy. However, there were also administrative responsibilities, including the apportionment that each parish had to pay to the Deanery. He did not carry out this and other tasks.

Eventually, it was agreed that he should move to Manea near March. The previous Bishop, Frederic Chase, wrote (23rd July 1925) 'It will be a very great change. Manea is almost the antithesis of Hemingford...' Francis moved there with his family in October 1925. As a lifelong naturalist, he began to supplement his income by journalism, writing Nature Notes for national newspapers and magazines under the pseudonym 'Marsh Harrier'. In 1940, he obtained a loan of £66 from Queen Anne's Bounty, repayable by ten annual instalments, to make improvements to the parsonage house.

Madeline increasingly handled their financial affairs, but he still needed to turn to his brother Teddie for loans. Life with him at Manea became increasingly difficult for Madeline, and in 1941 she left him and took the boys to live at Hartford, across the river from Hemingford. Thereafter she had little contact with him but corresponded with his nephew Dennis and his wife Elizabeth for the rest of their lives.

Their time in Manea was valued by many of the parishioners. In 1977, Madeline wrote to Dennis, who had just been there, 'How thrilled the people would be to have you (visit) and hear about Francis. They were so good to us all—such kind-hearted people—if they liked you.' On her 96th birthday in the following year, she had 'a galaxy of cards and several letters' from Manea.

Figure 49 Francis Falkner Herbert, c. 1950

Francis had served in the Observer Corps during the war, and subsequently, with his 'sharp mind and tongue', he contributed to the committees and subcommittees of the County Council and other councils as well as several charities. However, his personal life continued to deteriorate during this public service. The Rectory had become increasingly squalid, and he had allowed people to 'squat' in the Rectory who subsequently refused to move out. The Bishop of Ely was most concerned about his situation: 'He is in a pathetic state and feels very bitter…' After discussions and correspondence with Dennis, the Bishop accepted Francis's resignation in 1953.

After various further difficulties, Francis spent most of the last four years of his life in a British Legion home in Surrey. The six sons of Henry Herbert each had distinguished lives.[283] Francis was the last to die, in

[283] These were: Dennis 1869–1947; Edward 1870–1951; Louis 1873–1955; Richard 1874–1948; George 1876–1947; Francis 1879–1957 (Herbert, *Successive Journeys*, p. 99).

1957, aged 78. He was survived by his wife, who died in 1980, and his two sons.

Hugh Frith, Rector (1925–26)

Patrons: Representatives of the late Henry Herbert

Hugh Cokayne Frith was the youngest of eight siblings. He was born in Welby, Lincolnshire, on 12 August 1869, to William Armetriding Frith, Rector of Welby, and his wife Mary. The 'Cokayne' part of his name reflected his grandmother's inheritance from her uncle, a silk merchant whose children died before him. Her husband, the Rev. Edward Cokayne, added Frith to his name in recognition of this, and their descendants have retained the dual name, including the Rt Rev Michael, who retired as Bishop of Hereford in 2019.

Hugh Frith played in the cricket and football elevens at Radley College, leaving the school in 1888. He entered Trinity College, Cambridge, as a pensioner, in the Michaelmas Term 1888, proceeding BA in 1891 and MA in 1898. After training for the ministry at Cuddesdon, he was ordained deacon in the Chester diocese in 1893 and priest in 1894.

Before being appointed to Hemingford Abbots in 1925, he held curacies at St Thomas's, Stockport, Cheshire, 1893–96; Holy Trinity, Latimer Road, London, 1897–98; St John-the-Baptist, Longton, Staffordshire, 1899–1904; and St George's, Wolverhampton, 1904–6.

He married Rose Winifred Bradford in 1906. They had two children, William Arthur Cokayne Frith and John Cokayne Frith. He was briefly curate-in-charge of Hartshill with Basford, Staffordshire, 1906–7, before becoming Vicar of St Paul's, Bury, Lancashire, 1907–19; and then Vicar of Elsham, Lincolnshire, 1919–25.

He was Rector at St Margaret's for only a few weeks and died, following an operation, on 7 January 1926, at the age of 56.

The window on the south side of the chancel at St Margaret's is dedicated to his memory. The inscription is in red letters on a stone insert below the window, depicting a stylized sun: 'Truly the light is sweet, and a pleasant thing it is for the eyes to behold the sun' (Ecclesiastes 11:7).[284]

The opening of a window on the sunny south side of the Chancel made a significant difference to St Margaret's, as can be seen from Figure 40 and Figure 54. The window was dedicated to the memory of Hugh Frith on St Matthew's Day, 21st September 1932.

The crown glass in this window was installed by Chance of Smethwick, who were famous for the quality of glass required in lighthouses. Dr David Peace considered that this glass is a rare and fine example of its period.[285] The production of crown glass involved making a bubble of very fine blown glass, often with a slight curve. This was then cut in diamond shapes to make the most economical use of the smaller pieces of the glass. All the remainder went back into the furnace.

This may be a reference not only to lightening the chancel with this window, but also to the Cokayne-Frith crest. Incidentally, the communion silverware that he would have used has a round cartouche with a sunburst motif that was presented a century earlier and is inscribed: 'Church of St Margaret's, 1826'.[286]

Figure 50 Cokayne-Frith family crest

[284] This may be a reference not only to lightening the chancel with this window, but also to the Cokayne-Frith crest, which is described as 'above a grove of trees ppr., the sun in splendour or', James Fairbairn, *Fairbairn's Book of Crests of the Families of Great Britain and Ireland* (London: T. C. & E. C. Jack, 1905) http://archive.org/details/fairbairnsbookof01fair [accessed 17 February 2022], p. 123

[285] Cf. Charles Beresford and David Peace, *Hemingford Abbots Church: A Tour* (Hemingford Abbots, 2000, revised edition, 2007), p. 54.

[286] See Figure 33, p. 86, above.

It was unfortunate that Frith's incumbency was so short, in contrast to the fifty-eight years that his two predecessors, Henry and Francis Herbert, served the parish.

Figure 51 Frith memorial window

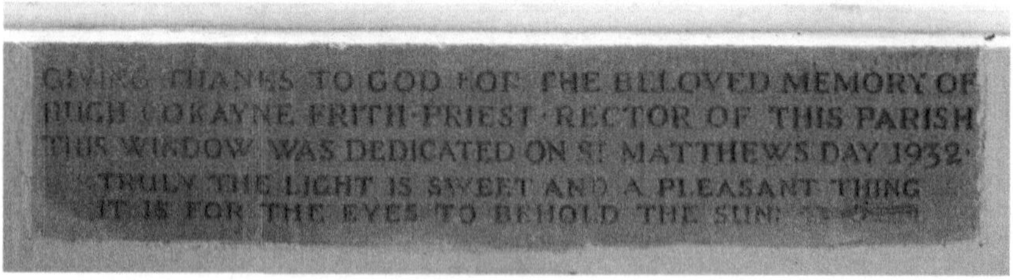

GIVING THANKS TO GOD FOR THE BELOVED MEMORY OF HUGH COKAYNE FRITH·PRIEST·RECTOR OF THIS PARISH. THIS WINDOW WAS DEDICATED ON ST MATTHEWS DAY 1932· TRULY THE LIGHT IS SWEET AND A PLEASANT THING IT IS FOR THE EYES TO BEHOLD THE SUN

Figure 52 Frith window inscription

Frank George, Rector (1926–30)

Patrons: Representatives of the late Henry Herbert

Figure 53 Frank Henry George

Frank Henry George was born on 4 December 1872 in Great Yarmouth. His father was a bookseller and a collector for the gas company. He was educated at Great Yarmouth School and won a scholarship to Jesus College, Cambridge, where he proceeded to his BA (second class, Classics Tripos) in 1893 and MA in 1909. He was ordained deacon in 1898 and priest in 1899 in the Diocese of St Albans. He spent much of his career in education, first as Assistant Master at Durston House School, Ealing, for two years; then at Berkhamsted School, Hertfordshire, 1898–1901. He was Chaplain of The Grange, Folkestone, a private preparatory school, 1901–6.

He was then at three of the Anglican Woodard Schools, first as an assistant master at Hurstpierpoint College, Sussex, 1906–13, then as Headmaster of King's College Taunton, 1913–19 during the First War, and as Headmaster of Bloxham in Oxfordshire, 1919–25.

In 1925, he returned to parish ministry, as Rector of Graveley, Huntingdonshire, a Jesus College living, where he served until 1926, before coming to Hemingford Abbots, aged 54, for five years, from 1926 to 1930.

The population of Hemingford Abbots declined from 372 in 1921 to 296 by 1931, less than the 306 that it had been in 1801. During George's incumbency, the church electoral roll reduced from 151 in 1927 to 134 in 1930; the number of school pupils fluctuated between 15 and 19, but there were 17 in both 1926 and 1930. The pupils left in the term in which they reached their eleventh birthday.

George visited the school in October 1926 soon after arriving and throughout his incumbency he visited the school on two or three mornings each week, checking the Register and taking the oldest children for Scripture lessons. In 1929 the Assistant Director of Education in the Diocese found that the children's scriptural knowledge was satisfactory, and they showed interest, and in 1930 the Diocesan Director of Education credited their good knowledge of facts and praised the accuracy of their repetition of the Catechism and the 'happy and sympathetic atmosphere' in the school. The HMI considered the school was improving, within the constraints of small numbers in each age group.

At his first PCC meeting, in November 1926, George was keen to revive the Parish Magazine and to improve the Rectory. No work had been carried out to make the Rectory fit for habitation since it was vacated in October 1925. Mr George's marriage to Violet Hawes in 1927 must have made the lack of progress particularly irksome to him.

The proposed reduction in the size of the Rectory required £250 to be raised by the parish to gain matching funding from the Ecclesiastical Commissioners and a grant from Queen Anne's Bounty.[287] Within a couple of weeks promises by the parishioners of nearly £170 were secured,

---

[287] https://en.wikipedia.org/wiki/Queen_Anne%27s_Bounty.

together with a loan guarantee to cover the balance. Further progress was delayed until dilapidations due from the previous incumbent had been paid or the Living mortgaged to Queen Anne's Bounty.

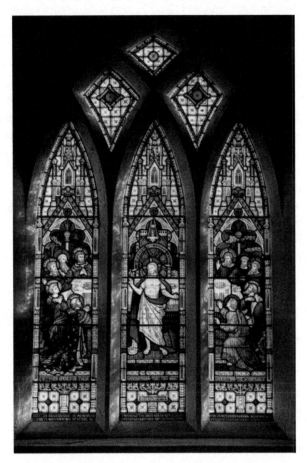

Figure 54 The Linton window

A window in the south aisle of the church blew in and needed replacing in 1927. Later in the year the roof of that aisle was leaking, and its restoration was sponsored by Mrs Jolliffe. In 1929 Mrs Williams also sponsored repairs to the north aisle, on condition that the PCC would improve the lighting and the heating. Furnishing of the south aisle was sponsored by Mrs Linton. The cleaning of the organ was completed in 1929. Plastering and distempering of the chancel and both aisles were to match the colour of the stone pillars in the nave.

The Linton window illustrates Christ with the gathering of the disciples in Jerusalem after the Resurrection (Luke 24: 33–51).[288] This followed his meeting with Cleophas and another disciple on the seven-mile road from Jerusalem to Emmaus and their return to Jerusalem after his blessing and disappearance (Luke 24: 13–31). Curiously, only ten of the eleven disciples 'and them that were with them', mentioned in verse 33, are shown in the window. Presumably Thomas and Judas are those omitted.

The Nativity window by Kempe & Company was installed in the north aisle in 1928.[289] Charles Kempe had died in 1907, but the manager of his renowned glass works in London was the master glass painter Alfred Tombleson (1851–1943), a son of the Houghton millwright. Tombleson retired to Hemingford Abbots, where he had bought the former 'Boot and Slipper' pub, initially as a holiday home.

Electric lighting was installed in 1930 and a 'Gurney' stove was installed by the west column of the north aisle, with the chimney going up and out through the clerestory wall. The Roman tomb or sarcophagus was moved to the west end of the north aisle.

[288] The stained glass by Clayton and Bell (1875) is a good example of the Gothic revival, based on the art of the 13th and early 14th centuries. There are similarities with John Clayton's earlier panel depicting the Ascension (1861) from St Peter the Great, Worcester. This is now displayed in the Stained Glass Museum at Ely Cathedral and illustrated in: Susan Mathews, Michael Archer, et al., *The Stained Glass Museum Gallery Guide* (Ely: The Stained Glass Museum, 2000), p. 18.

[289] Charles Kempe had worked with Clayton and Bell, who made the Resurrection window in the south aisle, before starting his own firm in 1869. After his death, in 1907, the firm passed to his nephew, Walter Tower, and a black tower, like a rook in chess, was added to the Kempe's wheatsheaf logo in the lower corners of their windows. Unfortunately, the Linton dedication replaced these logos when this window was installed. There are several other earlier local examples of Kempe windows locally, including Godmanchester (six between 1889 and 1914), Hilton (1896 and 1898), St Ives (1903), St Neots (1904), Hemingford Grey (1906), and Brampton (seven between 1917 and 1921). The firm ceased trading in 1934. See Stephen Day, *Stained Glass in Huntingdonshire: A Field Guide: An Exploration of the Figurative Stained Glass Windows in the Anglican Parish Churches of Huntingdonshire* (Crawley & Crawley, 2018), p. 64. Day, pp. 14, 15, 60, 64.

Figure 55 Jolliffe window, Kempe and Co., 1927

In 1930, an altar with appropriate furnishings was placed at the east end of the south aisle. This was donated by Mrs Linton in memory of Colonel Linton, who had been Churchwarden and Chairman of the School Managers. Colonel Sholto-Douglas[290] donated part of Figgis Meadow so that the churchyard could be extended northwards.

[290] Colonel Henry Mitchell Sholto-Douglas (1847 to 1931) was lord of the manors of Hemingford Abbots and Grey.

Figure 56 Watercolour of St Margaret's church before 1930

Frank George chaired the PCC and was also elected as secretary in 1929. At his last PCC meeting in 1930, The Patron, Mr Herbert, reported that the Bishop had approved the Trustees' nomination of the Rev. Algernon Ayre as the next Rector.

Mr George had been appointed as Rector of Brampton, Huntingdonshire, where he also served as Rural Dean, from 1930 to 1937. He then moved to Orton Longueville, 1937–40, and to Elton, 1940–44. Like Hemingford Abbots, both parishes are in Ely Diocese, despite being close to Peterborough. He retired back to his Norfolk home region and died five years later in Gorleston, aged 76, on 23 June 1949.

Algernon Ayre, Rector (1931–32)

Patrons: Representatives of the late Henry Herbert

Algernon Early Ayre was the third of four rectors at Hemingford Abbots between 1925 and 1935. He was born on 3 July 1872 in Sculcoates, Hull, Yorkshire. His father was an oilcake merchant and a J.P. He was educated at the Merchant Taylors' School and Wadham College, Oxford, where he was an exhibitioner. He graduated BA in 1894, with a third in theology, and proceeded MA in 1897.

He was ordained deacon in 1896 and priest in 1898 in Ripon Diocese. He held curacies in Yorkshire at Sharow (1896–99) and Richmond (1899–1904). He was then the domestic and examining chaplain to the Bishop of Ripon, William Boyd Carpenter, and Lecturer at Ripon Theological College, (1904–6).

Ayre's first incumbency was as Rector of Thornton-in-Craven, 1906–14. Hartley records: 'The Earby Church was erected in 1907, under the direction of the Rev. A. E. Ayre, who was specially commissioned by the Bishop of Ripon. In 1923, Earby was made into a separate ecclesiastical parish'.[291]

Also in 1907, he was initiated as a Freemason at the Craven Lodge and was on the register from 1910 to 1921 (Skipton 810/285).

In 1910, he married Agatha Sinclair (born 1884 in Hull, Yorkshire) and they had three children, Eleanor, Muriel, and William. Her aunt was the radical May Sinclair, who published twenty-one novels and several philosophical works between 1904 and 1927.[292]

Ayre served in Lincolnshire during the First World War, at Careby with Holywell and Aunby from 1914 to 1917, and then Toynton St Peter with All Saints near Spilsby, from 1917 to 1919. He moved back to Yorkshire as Vicar of Pateley Bridge in Nidderdale from 1919 to 1931.

Ayre came to Hemingford Abbots in 1931, aged 57. His first meeting with the Parochial Church Council was in March and included discussion about improving the heating and the training of the choir.

On 7 June, the spire was damaged by an earthquake and was considered to be in a dangerous condition but could be repaired by a

[291] J. Hartley, *Craven Herald*, 3 August 1934.
[292] Cf. Suzanne Raitt, *May Sinclair: A Modern Victorian* (Oxford: Clarendon Press, 2000).

steeplejack for £30. A free-will offering day raised £33 in 78 envelopes (£2,263 at 2020 values), which was sufficient to pay for the repairs to the steeple and the gilding of the clockface.

Ayre was asked to undertake the running of the annual tennis tournament in August, together with Mr Lewis Day and Sir Lionel Alexander. £14 was raised for the church funds. The Church Room was vacated by the British Legion and was taken over by the Parochial Church Council.

Other issues included the purchase of a second-hand safe, improvements to the porch, and the initiation of a churchyard committee to raise funds for its upkeep. The salary for the new organist was agreed at £20 (£1,371 at 2020 values), including transport costs, with terms and conditions defined.

Agatha Ayre was actively involved in the Hemingford Abbots Mothers' Union as the Chairman and Enrolling Member. The idea of the banner, which is still displayed in the north aisle of the church, was initiated and designed, and the ten guineas for it were raised while she was chairman. It was dedicated in July after her departure. She was presented with a fountain pen on 12 April 1932 by the members 'as a token of appreciation of her loving work and of their great regret at her departure after only one year.'

Figure 57 Mothers' Union banner, 1932

Mr and Mrs Ayre moved back to their native Yorkshire, where his successor at Thornton-in-Craven, J. T. Tanfield, left in 1932. The local paper reported in 1934 'Mr. Ayre has returned to the scene of his former clerical labours, to the great joy of his parishioners, who hold him in very high esteem.'

In 1941, Agatha was Gazetted as a Sister in Queen Alexandra's Imperial Military Nursing Service Reserve. In 1944, their only son William died, aged 24, when as a Flight Sergeant he was captaining a Lancaster bomber that was shot down.

Ayre was 72 in 1944. He died, aged 85, at Hermitage, Berkshire, on 16 April 1958. Mrs Ayre died in Berkshire in 1971, aged 87, and their daughter Muriel died in 1995, aged 81.

Julius Clements, Rector (1932–35)

Patrons: Representatives of the late Henry Herbert

Julius Clements-Frazer was born in the Wirral, Cheshire, in 1882, to James A. Frazer, a provisions broker's agent, and his wife Anne, both from Ireland. In the 1901 Census, he is recorded as living with his mother, the head of the household, and two siblings at 21 Clarendon Road, Bedford. His father was living in Liverpool while on business and was also listed there in the 1911 Census, as a widower.

He was educated at Bishop Hatfield's Hall, Durham, from which he graduated BA in 1905. He was ordained deacon in 1905 and priest in 1906 in the Chester Diocese. He held curacies at St Anne's, Birkenhead (1905–7) and Holy Trinity, Birkenhead (1908–9), where he was reported as having preached 'an excellent sermon.'

His reasons for changing his surname to 'Clements', his use of 'Clemence' in his signature, and his change to 'Jules' from 'Julius', are unclear. Similarly, his future wife became known as Nancy rather than Annie.

Clements moved to South Africa in 1909, where he was Priest-in-charge of St Philip's Mission, Bloemfontein (1909–10).[293] He then moved some 90 miles to be Priest-in-charge of St Matthew's, in a suburb of

---

[293] Arthur Chandler was Bishop of Bloemfontein from 1902 until 1920.

Kimberley in 1910–11.[294] Clements then became Vicar of Kenilworth, (1912–15); and Director of St Matthew's Mission, Kimberley (1911–16). He was appointed Diocesan Secretary and Director of Diocesan Education, Kimberley, from 1915 and was a Licensed Preacher in the Diocese of Kimberley (1916–32).

He married Annie Isabel Orchard (1877–1949) who had emigrated from Rugby to South Africa in 1903. Her first husband, Percy Martin Dickins (1875–1916), was killed in action on the Somme. She was listed in the *Women's Who's Who* (1934–35) as founder and Principal for 20 years of Kimberley Academic and Commercial School.

Clements returned to England in 1932 after 23 years living in South Africa. He was rector at Hemingford Abbots from 1932 to 1935. At his first quarterly meeting of the PCC in April, he reported that, on arrival, he had found the organist, Miss Unwin, was remaining only until the following Sunday. The PCC had declined to pay for a replacement while she took her annual two-week holiday. He persuaded her to remain until after Easter and agreed to take on the duties of Choirmaster with Miss Unwin as Organist for a while. Other organists were engaged subsequently, though Miss Unwin returned several years later to be organist and choirmaster for many years, despite living in Houghton.

Negotiations about the Rector's stipend, the sale of Glebe land, and paying for the rebuilding of the Rectory progressed during his incumbency. Several other issues also continued, such as the unsatisfactory heating of the church; the variable accuracy of the clock; the appointments, salary and conditions of the organists, and the maintenance of the churchyard. The PCC decided that the church should be locked at night.

Plans were developed to enlarge the sanctuary in the church, with the communion rails and steps moved west as far as the entrance to the vestry, the wooden platform being replaced by stone across the chancel from north to south. This was later tiled and is now carpeted.

---

[294] The neo-Gothic St Cyprian's church was dedicated in 1908 and became a cathedral in 1911 for the reorganized diocese of Kimberley and Kuruman. The first bishop, Wilfrid Gore-Browne, served from 1912 until his death in 1928. The chancel of the cathedral was completed in 1926. The dean of the cathedral, Thomas Robson, died in 1934 after serving St Cyprians as Rector of the parish and then Dean since 1905.

Changes to the timing of the services were agreed. Clements wanted to introduce the version of the Holy Communion that had been developed in the 1928 version of the Prayer Book, but the PCC wished to retain the traditional wording and placing of the prayer of oblation. This difference reflected a wider debate at the time. The Rector consented, but with the omission of the prayer of oblation. He stated that 'he had a ruling from the Bishop that the spiritual matters of the Parish were entirely in his hands.'

His final PCC meeting was in October 1935, when the council approved the plan for the Sholto-Douglas window on the south side of the south aisle with the inscription 'Suffer little children to come unto me.' The window includes the crowned red heart of Robert the Bruce, King of Scotland and Earl of Huntingdon.[295] This is a feature of the Douglas arms.

The stained glass in the Sholto-Douglas window was made in 1873 by Heaton, Butler and Bayne. Its style contrasts with the adjacent Resurrection scene, made two years later by Clayton and Bell.[296]

The two firms had shared a workshop between 1859 and 1861 'to the great benefit of both firms. Heaton and Butler brought technical excellence in glass production, and Clayton and Bell brought design excellence, not least from their highly talented designer Robert Bayne, who left them to go into partnership with Heaton and Butler in 1862.'[297]

---

[295] The medieval title of Earl of Huntingdon was associated for several centuries with the ruling house of Scotland. As Robert the Bruce lay dying of leprosy in 1329, he asked his trusted and favourite General Sir James Douglas to go on a pilgrimage to Jerusalem for him. Douglas took Robert's embalmed heart with him. In Andalucia, Spain, he was fighting in 1330 against the infidel Moors at Teba for King Alphonso of Castille. 'There he uttered the immortal words 'Jamais arrière' (Never behind) as he flung Bruce's heart forward into the melee.' Oliver Thomson, *From the Bloody Heart: The Stewarts and the Douglases* (History Press, 2003), p. 19. The heart was retrieved and returned to Scotland, where it is interred at Melrose Abbey. 'It became the badge of the Douglas family and one of the inspirations behind years of plotting to undermine the kings of Scotland' (Thomson inscription).

[296] See footnote 286, above.

[297] Day, p. 64.

Figure 58 Sholto-Douglas window

The heart is also included, together with the arms of Ramsey Abbey, in the village signs designed by David Peace (cf. Figure 9, p. 15, below). The Lordship of the Manor continues with the Sholto-Douglas family, though the land was sold in 1928-33.[298]

[298] The Sholto Douglas estate was sold in 1928–33, mainly in two auctions in 1930 and 1933 at the Corn Exchange, St Ives. 460 acres were sold in 1930 and 671 acres in 18 lots in 1933. The auctioneer on both occasions was HW Dean. 'Mr Bidwell of Cambridge had acted as agent for the estate, assisted by HW Dean in matters such as the annual stocktaking valuations. The properties comprised Lattenbury Farm, Topfield farm, Goretree farm, a number of fields, part of Hemingford Abbots meadow, part of Hemingford Grey meadow, the south-west half of Houghton Island, several building sites, the Manor House, Hemingford Abbots and various cottages. All of these properties were situated in and adjoining the

Figure 59 Sholto-Douglas window, detail

At his last Annual Meeting in 1935, Clements mentioned that, among the valuable contributions many people made to the life of the parish church, 'the League of Youth, in the charge of Mrs Clements, was still flourishing and proving a most beneficial factor among the younger members of the congregation.'

Mrs Nancy Clements also served as Enrolling Member and then Chairman of the Hemingford Abbots Mothers' Union.[299] She spoke at the December 1934 meeting on 'Some habits and customs of the native women of South Africa'. In May 1935 members attended the Mothers'

villages of Hemingford Abbots and Hemingford Grey. The two sales by auction were held respectively by direction of Colonel H. M. S. Douglas and HJ Sholto Douglas.' (Some of the lots were sold privately before the auctions.) H. W. Dean, *Life's Survey: My Working Life*, ed. Charles Beresford [son-in-law] (privately printed, 1993), chapter 42. Col. Sholto Douglas of Springfield Farm was the last Lord of the Manor to live in the village. His bailiff lived in the Manor House. The auction details are recorded in: *The remaining portions of the Hemingford Estate*, 12 June 1933.

[299] The Minutes of the Hemingford Abbots Branch of the Mothers' Union: vol. 1, up to 1930 is missing; vol. 2, April 1930 to June 1940; It is not known if the branch met between 1940 and 1956; vol. 3 or 4 from 1956 to 1966. The record books were passed to CB by Doris Bilton in 2017.

Union Festival at Manea at the invitation of Rev and Mrs Herbert, on the occasion of their silver wedding anniversary. In June 14 members went to Ely Cathedral and joined about 2000 others at a choral festival service. Mrs Linton was elected to bear the banner. Teas and open gardens perhaps encouraged the Mothers' Union festival to include some open gardens in the following month in Hemingford Abbots. Miss Joyce Clements helped with the teas. She was Nancy's 'incapacitated' daughter (1914–84), who lived with them in South Africa, Hemingford Abbots, and subsequently when they moved to Birchencliffe, Huddersfield in 1935.

In 1939, Clements was Vicar there and served as an Air Raid Warden during the war. Ten years later, he was at 37 Whitecoat Rise, Bramley, Leeds when he died, aged 67, in July 1949. His widow, Nancy, died four months later in November, aged 72.

Robert Balleine, Rector (May 1936–46)

Patrons: Representatives of the late Henry Herbert

Figure 60 Robert Wilfred Balleine

Robert Wilfred Balleine was born on 1 January 1881 in Bletchington, Oxfordshire, where his father, George Orange Balleine, was Rector. George later became Dean of Jersey, where he occupied a prominent place in society. The Balleine family had lived in Jersey since the 14th century.

Robert was educated at Victoria College in Jersey before attending Pembroke College, Oxford, where he was an exhibitioner and gained a first in mathematics in 1900, followed by a second in theology at Wycliffe Hall, Oxford in 1902. He graduated BA in 1903 and proceeded MA in 1906. He was ordained deacon in 1904 and priest in 1905 by Rt Rev. Edmund Knox, the Bishop of Manchester. He held curacies in Manchester at St. Paul's, Chorlton-on-Medlock, from 1904 to 1906, and St. Paul's, Astley Bridge, from 1906 to 1907. He was Domestic Chaplain to the Bishop of Manchester (1907–10) and Honorary Domestic Chaplain (1910–20).[300] He served as Diocesan Inspector of Schools for Manchester Diocese from 1910 to 1914. 'He did not inspect schools' educational standards, his job was to decide how effective they were as church schools, and to make sure a Christian ethos was maintained.[301]

Robert had an older brother, two older sisters, and two younger brothers. The brother closest in age to Robert was Cuthbert, later Fellow and Sub-Dean of Exeter College, Oxford. He was killed in action at Ypres on 2 July 1915. Robert and his other two brothers were all ordained. George was a priest in Bermondsey, London. Austin was a priest in Wakefield and was Domestic Chaplain to the Bishop of Wakefield. Austin and Robert both served as Chaplains to the Forces during the First

---

[300] Cf. 'The prominent evangelical Bishop Rt Rev Edmund Knox was one of only six bishops who voted in favour of allowing clergy to volunteer as combatants, contrasting with 19 who voted against (Bishop's meeting BM6 Oct 1915 Lambeth Palace Library). 'My heart is with those clergy who wish to show that they are ready to share the same hardships and dangers as the rest of their parishioners' he wrote in the Manchester Diocesan Magazine in May 1918 (quoted in Wikipedia entry on Edmund Knox). Robert must have made a good impression on Knox because after his three years supporting him, both as a priest and as an assistant, he was made an Honorary Domestic Chaplain for the remaining eleven years that Knox was in office.' (Museum of the Manchester Regiment: The men behind the medals: Robert Balleine), http://www.themenbehindthemedals.org.uk/index.asp?page=full&mwsquery=({Person%20identity}={Balleine,%20RW}).

[301] Ibid.

World War. As well as being religious leaders, their role was to provide friendship and morale-enhancing support. Each was decorated for bravery, Robert with an MC and Austin with an OBE.

Robert had twelve-month contracts each year between 1914 and 1919. He served with the Manchester Regiment on the front line in the trenches. A soldier later wrote: 'Day after day he went round the front line, sniped at and shelled like the rest of us, but never turning a hair. His pockets bulged with packets of cigarettes for the troops, and he had a cheery word for everyone.' It was reported that Robert had 'again and again' proved himself to be 'one of the bravest men in the Battalion'. In 1918 he was Senior Chaplain to the Forces in the 9th Division, ranking equivalent to Major. His bravery, particularly during the Somme offensives, was recognized with the award of the Military Cross. He returned to the UK in April 1919 and left the army in November, remaining an Honorary Chaplain to the Forces during his parish work. His four medals were presented to the Museum of the Manchester Regiment in 1973.

After the war, he held three incumbencies before coming to Hemingford Abbots. From 1919 to 1924, he was Rector of Heaton, Mersey. Then he served at St. Crispin's, Withington, Manchester (1924–30), where his brother Austin was curate. The family funded the development of a new vicarage, and the brothers lived there with their sister. A new church was developed, following fundraising efforts.

In 1931, he was appointed Vicar of Temple Balsall, Solihull, in the Diocese of Birmingham. There was some controversy over his appointment to Temple Balsall, an incumbency which included the Mastership of the Foundation of Lady Katherine Leveson, a Christian charity since 1674. The parish, which has historical links with the Knights Templar from the twelfth century, had developed a tradition of sung Eucharistic worship. This did not find favour with some parishioners, being regarded as too elaborate and high church. Balleine came from a new parish, which had developed catholic tendencies. At his Induction, the Bishop of Birmingham expressed a desire that the congregation welcome the new Vicar and appealed for harmony.

IN AID OF ST. CRISPIN'S CHURCH.

Rev. R. W. BALLEINE, *Rector.* The LORD BISHOP OF MANCHESTER Rev. A. H. BALLEINE, *Curate.*
Saturday, March 21st, 1926. (Dr. Temple.) [Daily Dispatch Phot.

Figure 61 Robert Balleine, William Temple, Austin Balleine

Five years later, in 1936, Balleine came to Hemingford Abbots. He soon discovered much about the history of the village and at Christmas 1936, produced his first 'Occasional Paper' with several interesting details about Hemingford Abbots, Christmas customs, and a quiz about details in the church. He was much involved with the Church School and the Glebe lands, especially Top Farm and Rectory Farm. A reference in 1939 in the local press reported his involvement as an official in the Regatta, otherwise he was not mentioned in the press during his incumbency.

Changes to the sanctuary were being carried out when he arrived. The floor had been retiled and the altar rails moved forward. There were new altar hangings and furnishings, including riddel posts and a silver cross, made from items that had been melted down, given by Mrs Edith Williams. The previous brass cross was given to the British Columbia and Yukon Church Aid Society for the Diocese of Cariboo. In 1937, a new altar was given anonymously, and in the following year, he and Mrs Williams gave two silver candlesticks.

In the 1939 Census, he is recorded as 'single', living at the Rectory in Hemingford Abbots, together with the schoolteacher, Percy Francis, and Percy's daughter, Olive, a scholar. A housekeeper and parlour maid are also listed.

In 1939, a portion of the Rectory paddock was sold to him to build a bungalow. In 1942, he proposed giving the freehold of the bungalow to the PCC, but this posed legal difficulties. It was given to Queen Anne's Bounty for the benefit of future incumbents.

He and the PCC wrote a letter of sympathy to the farmers in the parish when their stock was affected by an outbreak of Foot and Mouth disease in the summer of 1945. Rationing prevented the distribution of Charity Coal that Christmas. In January 1946, German prisoners of war were working in the churchyard, and volunteers were cleaning the chancel, vestry, and side-chapel and polishing the silver and brass.

It would appear that, like many incumbents, he regarded the post as a form of semi-retirement. He cared for the parish from 1936 until 1946, when he was 65—one of the longer twentieth-century incumbencies. His generosity to the church encouraged others. He drafted a history of St Margaret's, but no copy has been found.

After leaving Hemingford Abbots, he lived at Crosby Cottage, St Helen's, Isle of Wight, which he referred to as a 'tiny' house. He was granted permission to officiate in the Diocese of Portsmouth. In 1948, he wrote that he was in charge of the parish of Brading during an interregnum. Taking three services each Sunday involved travelling forty miles.

He remained unmarried and died in the year after his brother Austin, on 20 August 1951, at Moorfield's Eye Hospital, London. He was interred in Hemingford Abbots but has no headstone. His elder brother, the Rev. George Balleine, survived him in Jersey until 1966.

Reign of Edward VIII
(June 1936–December 1936)

No appointments were made.

Reign of George VI (1936–52)

Herbert Denison, Rector (1946–55)

Patrons: Representatives of the late Henry Herbert

Herbert Bouchier Wiggins was born in 1885, the ninth of twelve siblings, in Watlington, Oxfordshire, to parents William Wiggins, a farmer, and his wife Arabella.[302] He changed his surname by deed poll in 1910 to Denison, the maiden name of his mother, retaining Wiggins as his third forename.[303] He was educated at Magdalen College School and Brasenose College, Oxford, from which he graduated BA in 1906, MA in 1910.

His ministry training was at Newcastle-on-Tyne in 1907. He was ordained deacon in 1908 and priest in 1909 in the Newcastle Diocese. In 1908, he was appointed Curate of Benwell, Newcastle-on-Tyne. In 1910, he married Alice Dorothy Taylor, who had been born in Calcutta. From 1911–13, he served in Worsley with Ellenbrook and Winton.

He then moved south to Bedfordshire, where back in 1875 a maternal relative, the Rev. William Henry Denison, had purchased the advowson of Carlton, near Sharnbrook, with Chellington. The First World War began in the following year, and he served from 1915 to 1917 as a temporary forces Chaplain. During the ten years between 1913 and 1923. He is also recorded in 1922 as being an assistant master at Bedford Modern School.

He was then Vicar of Christ Church, Luton, from 1923 to 1925, before moving to West Sussex as Rector of Clayton with Keymer, where the living was in the gift of his college, Brasenose, Oxford. He was then Rector of Bexhill-on-Sea. He and Alice had two sons. He was a freemason and was an accomplished croquet player, as were other members of his family.[304]

Denison was 61 when he was instituted as Rector of Hemingford Abbots in November 1946, with an income of £400, the equivalent of £17,132 in 2020. This was raised to £500 in the following year, equivalent to £20,007 in 2020. Mrs Denison replaced Mr Payne as organist. The organ-blower's wages were raised from 13 shillings to £1 per quarter, equivalent to £40 in 2020.

---

[302] 1891 Census, Watlington, Oxfordshire.

[303] His mother, Arabella Annie (Denison) Wiggins (1845–1926) died 16 years later.

[304] Several of his croquet matches at county level were reported in regional newspapers, e.g., *Gloucestershire Echo*, 21 July 1938, 'The Cheltenham Championship Handicap Doubles Third Round. — Rev. H. B. W. Denison and Mrs. C. Waydelin … beat I I. Case and J. A. C. Younger … E. M. Hunt … beat Rev. H. B. W. Denison …'

The parish faced a variety of practical challenges in the post-war years, some of which are referred to in the records of PCC meetings. For example, the extreme winter of 1947 brought the inadequacy of the church heating system to a head. Mr Denison and Mr Bowles put up a curtain of balloon fabric across the west archway into the tower for £6. It was replaced six years later by an oak and glass screen to commemorate the Coronation. This was funded by part of a generous bequest from Mrs Williams of Barn Hall.

Also in the winter of 1947, the river burst its banks, and the Rector delivered coal in a punt. The church and the rectory house were among the few buildings not flooded or affected. A fund-raising event for replacing the heating system was organized in May—an afternoon fete at Hemingford Park with sideshows, a flower show, and boxing competition. A bus transported people from the centre of the village to the Park. In the evening a dance was held on the Rectory Lawn. The event raised over £222, equivalent to £8,883 today.

The old church stoves were replaced with a hot air heating system for £277, and another fete was held in the following summer. This raised £96, which paid off the remainder of the heating bill and enabled the organ to be improved, including the installation of an electric blower. Annual fetes followed, which, Denison said at the 1949 annual meeting, were 'desirable as social events and necessary from a financial point of view'.

There were about 340 residents in 1947. By 1961, this had increased to 628. While he was rector, the electoral roll increased from 113 in 1947 to 154 in 1953. He was involved in several improvements, such as the installation of the new pulpit and the repairs to the steeple in 1950. As well as chairing and motivating the active PCC, Denison carried out many practical tasks, including using his motor scythe in the churchyard. He was in regular contact with the village school.

Figure 62 Pulpit, installed 1950

The Church Commissioners sold the Rectory in 1949 to Dennis Herbert, grandson of Henry Herbert. He succeeded his father as Baron Hemingford in 1947 and was retiring from his distinguished roles in education in Africa.[305] Denison is reported to have been the driving force behind the building of the new thatched council houses in Rideaway Drive in the 1950s, at which time he was a Rural District Councillor in St Ives.[306]

He was also involved with the Patrons and the PCC in the decisions to sell the old rectory in 1949 and two years later to resist the compulsory purchase of Top Farm and to raise a loan to improve both that and Rectory Farm. The wartime Agricultural Committee had requisitioned two of the farm cottages from 1942 to 1947, and Italian prisoners of war were

[305] Correspondence relating to the Africa Bureau 1952–71 is at the Bodleian Library, Oxford, MSS Afr s 1681, 1712–14.

[306] An interesting article in the Peterborough Advertiser mentioning Denison's desire 'to preserve the old world charm of one of the most beautiful villages in Huntingdonshire' was published on 29 April 1955, p. 9.

billeted there. In 1947, the cottages were derelict, and all the woodwork, including staircases, had been torn away and burnt. However, these were the Rector's freehold. The improvements would cost £3,000 but would generate £427 annual rental after costs. With other income, this would raise the income of the living to £816 (approx. £26,000 today).

On 26 January 1952, he wrote to Col. Herbert: 'it is very much my hope that I may be able to leave everything connected with the living in shipshape order with a reasonable income. The church itself is in splendid order, with the repair to the steeple costing £400 completed and paid for. I am afraid on the spiritual side I shall never be able to render so good an account. There, I must confess, the general condition of things is far from satisfactory.'

The advowson transferred from the last of Henry Herbert's sons, Willie and Francis, to his grandson Dennis, 2nd Lord Hemingford, in 1954. In a letter, dated 20 May 1954, Francis Herbert wrote to Dennis: 'It was always Aunt Carrie's [Caroline Herbert] wish that the Living might be kept in the Herbert family … at one time she wished to leave everything to the benefice to augment the value of the Living so long as it was held by a member of the family … I hope the advowson may long remain in the Herbert family.'

Denison retired, after nine years as Rector, in November 1955, aged 70. The PCC noted 'various unofficial duties had been carried out by the Rector. Offers of help were made by members of the council to undertake these jobs.'

He died at the College of St Barnabas, a home for retired clergy, in Lingfield, Surrey, on 29 August 1966.

Reign of Elizabeth II (1952–)

James Stevens, Rector (1955–61)

Patron: Dennis, 2nd Lord Hemingford

James Reginald Stevens was the youngest of six siblings, born on 26 October 1882, in Farnham, Surrey. His father was James E. Stevens (1847–1908), and his mother was Florence, née Julius (1846–1937). Stevens graduated from Lincoln College, Oxford, in 1906, took his MA in 1916, and was articled as a solicitor in his father's law practice in Castle Street, Farnham.

In 1920, aged 38, he decided to train for the ministry, as his grandfather before him had done. He studied at Ridley Hall, Cambridge, a training college on the evangelical wing of the Church. He was ordained priest in 1921 in Nagpur, India, and became assistant master at the Boys' High School, Panchgani, 1922–23 and Mt Abu 1923–24. He returned briefly to England, teaching at Forest School, Walthamstow in 1925–26. Then from 1927–36 he was Principal of St Matthew's Boys' School, Moulmein, Burma (now Mawlamyine, Myanmar).

Returning to England, he served as curate in several parishes from 1936 to 1944, when he became Vicar of St Peter's, Wrecclesham, near Farnham. His maternal grandfather, the Rev. Henry Julius (1816–91), had been involved in building the church there when he was Curate at St Andrew's, Farnham. Julius had then served as the Vicar at Wrecclesham for 40 years from 1846 to 1886. He baptized James there on 3 December 1882.[307]

Henry Julius's daughter, Florence Julius, later James Stevens's mother, was born in the year that her parents moved to Wrecclesham. She was one of Henry Julius's ten children and enjoyed a happy childhood there, according to her notebook, which was later published.[308] When her father died in 1891, she was 45, and her son James was 11.

James was ordained thirty years later in 1921. After returning from India to England in 1936, he eventually returned to Wrecclesham as its priest in 1944. One of his parishioners was Carlotta Marion Strachey, who was born in Moradabad, Bengal on 9 September 1895. Marion and her widowed mother Ann were living in Wrecclesham until Ann died, aged 79, in 1951.

In 1952, aged 70, James married Marion, who was 57. James and Marion Stevens lived in Wrecclesham for three years after their marriage. In 1955, they came to Hemingford Abbots. Denison, his predecessor, announced his retirement to the PCC in July. Stephens was inducted in November.

In the following April, he reintroduced a Parish Magazine, which sold for threepence each month throughout his incumbency. In the first issue, he wrote: 'Owing mainly to severe weather and somewhat

[307] John Birch and Roy Waight, 'Old Julius' https://www.farnhammuseumsociety.org.uk/Old_Julius.htm [accessed 3 November 2021].
[308] Farnham Museum Society, 'To the Vicarage Born'.

prolonged bad health I have not yet visited quite all parishioners, but I have been to some 90%. At every house, whether belonging to Church-goers or not, I have received a most kind and a warm invitation to 'come in'. Perhaps you can hardly realize what a difference this makes to a Rector's work, and (believe me!) it is not always thus!'

Mr and Mrs Stevens were soon fully integrated into village life. They lived in the Rectory bungalow, which is now a private home and was adjacent to the school. It had been built in 1939 and was the home of the incumbents until 1964.

Stevens maintained the traditional, broad-church worship at St Margaret's with four services each Sunday — Holy Communion at 8:30, Mattins at 11:00, Children at 2:30, and Evensong at 6:30. The numbers on the electoral roll declined from 153 in 1955 to 136 in 1957, but then stabilized at 130 in 1961. The village was growing significantly during the 1950s, from 348 in 1951 to 628 in 1961, the same as in the 2011 Census.

Stevens paid frequent visits to the Church School and chaired the Managers. He developed a good relationship with the Headteacher, Mrs Blanche Cornell (1947–68), and her daughter, Mrs Penelope Yeandle, who taught there from 1959 to 1978.[309] He allowed the Rectory garden to be used by the children for dancing and other activities. Her Majesty's Inspector of Schools gave the school an excellent report on 27 June 1961. There were 33 children in 1961 and 37 in 1962.

Morning service was broadcast on the BBC Home Service on 21 October 1956, as it had been in the previous year, beginning with the church bells.[310] In 1959, the choir took part in a festival of music at St Albans, and some robes were bought in the following year.

Mrs Stevens revived the branch of the Mothers' Union in October 1956 and was the Chairman and enrolling member. Its active programme is recorded in the Minute Book. She also launched a Sunday School, whose three young teachers went to summer schools. These developments were considered very successful, as was the 'Church

[309] See https://www.hemlocs.co.uk/Abbotsschool.html.

[310] The PCC Minutes of 14 December 1956 record that Mr Stevens had obtained a long-playing record of this broadcast. The *Radio Times* (issue 1719, p. 10) showed that this broadcast at 9:30 a.m. on Education Sunday was conducted by the Rector, the Rev J. R. Stevens; that the preacher was Lord Hemingford and the organist G. S. Short. The service included four hymns and the psalm for the day.

Fellowship' started by Mr Brookes. Other improvements during Stevens's six-year chairmanship of the PCC included monthly Family Services; rewiring of the lighting; conversion of the heating from solid fuel to oil; installation of piped water and a tap in the churchyard for the Flower Guild.

The PCC Minutes and Parish Magazines record many aspects of a typical village parish at the time, such as a tree planting scheme for the churchyard; replacing hymn and chant books; reviving the clock's striking mechanism; maintaining the organ and bells; fund raising at Church fetes and the Bishop preaching.

Stevens retired at the age of 79 in 1961, in which year Hemingford Abbots won the Best-Kept Village Competition. He and his wife moved to Saltdean, Brighton. He died, aged 89, on 17 June 1971, and she died in 1991, both in Rottingdean, Sussex.

Figure 63 St Margaret's choir, c. 1952[311]

[311] The date is uncertain but thought to be c. 1952. Back row (left to right): Maureen Clifton; unknown; 'Molly' Nickson (née Mary Chapman, 1915–92); Edith 'Edie' Saunders, b. 1903; June Gowler; unknown; Front row: Janice Nickson, b. 1942; Pauline Saunders, b. 1941; Phyllis Perkins; Chris Wynn; unknown; Pamela Saunders, b. 1941; Dorothy Gowler.

Ernest Bawtree, Rector (1961–76)

Patron: Dennis, 2nd Lord Hemingford

Figure 64 Ernest Bawtree, 1974[312]

---

[312] Bishop of Ely, Edward Keymer Roberts, left; Henry Myles Herbert (son of Francis, grandson of Henry Herbert), right.

Ernest Anderson Bawtree was born on 30 July 1906 in Wallington, Surrey. He was the fourth of five sons born to Percy Bawtree and his wife, Margaret Anderson, from whom he took his second Christian name. His father, Percy, was an insurance clerk, and his grandfather, Samuel, had been a member at Lloyds of London. After working in London for a couple of years he gained 'a solid grounding in theology' in 1925–27 at the Bible Training Institute in Glasgow — 'two years of porridge and psalms', as he later put it.[313] After a further year at the London Missionary School of Medicine, he was accepted by the Africa Inland Mission and sailed for Arua, Uganda, in 1928. Following a two-year course of reading and an examination, he was ordained deacon in 1932. Back in England, he attended the Colonial course at the London Institute of Education, joined the Church Missionary Society and returned to Uganda in 1934 to train teachers at Mukono.

Figure 65 Ernest Bawtree, 1934 (aged 28)[314]

Returning to England in 1938, he was Chaplain to Queen Mary's Hospital for Sick Children in Carshalton as a curate for the Vicar of Wallington. He returned to Uganda and followed another course of reading and

[313] Letter to Lord Hemingford, 5 May 1961,

[314] https://westnilechurchhistory.wordpress.com/, q.v. for details of his missionary activity in Africa.

examination, after which he was ordained priest in Namirembe Cathedral Kampala in 1947, under the Colonial Clergy Act.

He served in Uganda for twenty-seven years, including being Archdeacon of Toro (Ton-Buyoo-Mboga) in Ruwenzori diocese. He also held other administrative posts, including Secretary of the Diocesan Council and District Commissioner for Scouts.

He retired from Uganda in 1961 and came to Hemingford Abbots, aged 56. He was a friend, from their time together in Uganda, of Dennis, 2nd Lord Hemingford, the Patron. He was the first incumbent to live in the newly built Rectory house, designed by Trevor Roberts.[315] David Peace designed East-African cranes in glass panels along the landing in the Rectory. These have not survived *in situ*, but the previous Diocesan Secretary assured Ven. Richard Sledge that they were safe.[316]

Ernest Bawtree's incumbency was remarkable for its length and success. He was the last full-time incumbent of St Margaret's and devoted himself fully to the welfare of the church and local community. He was no innovator but ensured that things ran smoothly and without fuss. Although his upbringing had favoured evangelicalism, his theology and broad churchmanship embraced the preferences of those from different backgrounds. His friendly, sincere manner inspired much affection in the village and further afield. From 1965 to 1971, he took three services each Sunday: Holy Communion at 8:30. Matins at 11:00, and Evensong at 6:30.

In May 1971, a half-hour informal 'Children's Church' in the Lady Chapel was added at 10:00 and flourished during his incumbency, replacing the previous Sunday School. On his retirement, David Peace inscribed a glass panel with the signatures of 51 children who currently came to the Children's Church and had also known Mr Bawtree through his regular visits to the school. This is displayed alongside the Douglas

[315] In a note of 29 June 1960, the secretary of the Ely Diocesan Board of Dilapidations wrote: 'Vicarages and Rectories … are often millstones when they should be cornerstones.' The new rectory attracted a 50% grant towards the £7,000 cost from the Church Commissioners, and the parsonage bungalow next to the school was sold when the new Rectory was completed.

[316] Diocesan Secretary Dr Matthew Lavis, letter to the Ven. Richard Sledge, 3 December 2004.

window in the south aisle, which has the caption 'Suffer little children to come unto me.'

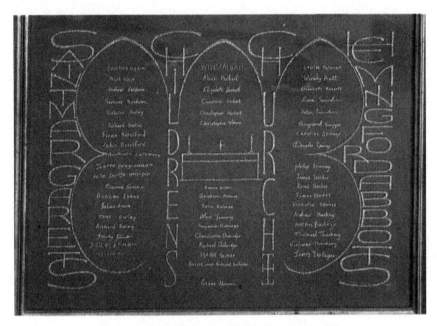

Figure 66 Children's church inscription[317]

Attendance numbers were steady, with his meticulous records showing a slight upward trend. His sermons were prepared with much thought and always written out in specially prepared booklets. The style and

[317] Joanne Aston, Mark Aston, Andrew Baldwin, Susan Baldwin, Nicolas Bentley, Richard Bentley, Fiona Beresford, John Beresford, Amanda Casemore, Joanne Doidge-Harrison, Kate Doidge-Harrison, Claire Evans, Duncan Evans, Julian Evans, Jane Ewing, Richard Ewing, Timothy Fawcett, Bradley Hall, Leslie Hall, William Hall, Alice Herbert, Elizabeth Herbert, Caroline Herbert, Christopher Herbert, Christopher Wilson, Emma Wilson, Graham Holmes, John Holmes, Alan January, Benjamin Newbridge, Christopher Newbridge, Rachel Newbridge, Isobel Palmer, Robert and Richard Sullivan, Grace Unwin (Organist), Louise Palmer, Wendy Pratt, Elizabeth Roberts, Fiona Sanderson, Raymond Sawyer, Caroline Spinney, Douglas Spinney, Philip Spinney, James Stocker, Karen Stocker, Simon Stocker, Victoria Squires, Andrew Thackray, Martin Thackray, Michael Thackray, Nicholas Thackray, James Verlaque.

delivery of his deep voice, which would from time to time rise in pitch, through excitement, were notable for their sincerity and measured quality. He encouraged younger people, for example in the Children's service, in the choir, and in well-attended confirmation groups. His ministry extended also to caring for young offenders at the nearby Borstal Institution, Gaynes Hall. His manner was friendly and unassuming, possibly with a slightly unworldly quality at times. Although he was a canon and had been an archdeacon, he never used the titles nor called himself 'Venerable'.

He had two dogs—Jasper and Gypsy—which he could be seen walking through the village at regular times, with the dogs tugging him forwards on the leash. He served as a parish councillor and was thoroughly involved in village activities. His passion was collecting modern art. He filled the Rectory with paintings by artists such as Kit Barker which he acquired from London galleries, and he greatly enjoyed talking about them to visitors.

He employed the school cook, Mrs 'Molly' Nickson, as his part-time housekeeper. Her husband, Reg Nickson, served as Churchwarden for many years and carried out numerous practical maintenance tasks in the church.

He retired, in 1976, to a bungalow for retired clergy in Bishop Wynn Close, Ely, and enjoyed a new lease of life, ministering part-time in the Cathedral and attending St Mary's Church. He died in Ely Cathedral on 30 October 1988. His ashes are interred in St Margaret's churchyard, strewn on the south side near the Douglas window in a cruciform shape and marked by a simple granite tablet. Lord Hemingford's article about him in the Parish Magazine is a fine tribute spanning his years in Uganda and Hemingford Abbots.[318]

---

[318] Nicholas Herbert, 'A Tribute to Canon Ernest Anderson Bawtree', *Hemingford Abbots Parish Magazine*, February 1989 and *Scallop*, Hemingford Grey Parish Magazine, March 1989.

David Young, Rector (1977)

Patron: Dennis, 2nd Lord Hemingford

Figure 67 David Young

David Young was appointed in 1977. The son of a brigadier in the Indian army, he was born on 2 September 1931 in India. After attending Wellington College in Berkshire, a school with strong military connections, he did his national service as a second lieutenant in the Royal Engineers. He then went up to Balliol College, Oxford, where he gained a first class degree in Mathematics. He worked as a research mathematician with Plessey before studying for the priesthood at Wycliffe Hall, Oxford. Following curacies in Liverpool and London, he studied Sanskrit and Pali at the School of Oriental and African Studies, University of London, before going to Sri Lanka with the Church Missionary Society. He became Director of Buddhist Studies at Lanka Theological College in Kandy, returning to England in 1967, following the death of his first wife, Rachel (née Lewis) in a car crash. He then lectured in Buddhist Studies at Manchester University and married Jane Havill.

In 1970, he was appointed Vicar of Burwell and lectured part-time in the Divinity Faculty at Cambridge University. From 1972, he was a chaplain in the Territorial Army until his appointment as Archdeacon of Huntingdon and Vicar of Great Gidding in 1975.

Young was Rector of Hemingford Abbots for only a few months, from January to September in 1977. He was then elevated to the episcopacy as Bishop of Ripon and thus left the parish unexpectedly soon. The only previous Rector of Hemingford Abbots to become a bishop was Lawrence Booth, who became Bishop of Durham in 1448 and subsequently Lord High Chancellor and Archbishop of York.

Young had been Archdeacon of Huntingdon for two years when he arrived at Hemingford Abbots, following Ernest Bawtree's retirement after fifteen years as Rector. The Diocese of Ely wished to locate the Archdeacon of Huntingdon in Hemingford Abbots, since it was a small, well-situated parish, which would enable the incumbent to devote his time principally to archdeaconry matters.

He arrived at Hemingford Abbots in 1977 and, with the approval of the PCC, immediately set about introducing changes.

Although this is generally acknowledged as a dangerous thing for a new incumbent to do, Young did so in a sympathetic and sensitive way. The pattern of Sunday services was altered from the threefold 8:30 Holy Communion, 11:00 Matins, and 6:30 Evensong, to either 8:30 Holy Communion and 10:00 Matins, or 10:00 Parish Eucharist and 6:30 Evensong, or on the fifth Sunday of the month, 10:00 Family Service and 6:30 Parish Eucharist. The weekly 'Children's Church', formerly a separate service, was to be integrated into the main Sunday service for part of the time.

Young's approach was to modernize and consolidate, whilst trying to draw the various strands of the church family closer together. He wrote in the *Parish Magazine*: 'I would ask all of you to support this new pattern, not by attending the services which you like but by coming regularly each Sunday even if the service is not your personal choice.' His evangelical leanings led him to adopt a different style and to introduce contemporary-language services, together with John Rutter's setting of 'Series 3' for the Eucharist.

He discontinued the use of Eucharistic vestments, which had been the tradition of the church for many years. His justification of this was that the vestments were so old and inferior as to be no longer serviceable. It was his declared intention to purchase new ones, had he stayed longer.

He was generally sympathetic to the traditions of the church, and people were largely at ease with the changes that he introduced. He and his wife made friends quickly and easily in the village. He had five children.

When an incumbent is elevated to the episcopacy, the patronage and right of appointment of the next incumbent pass temporarily to the Monarch. David Young was succeeded as Rector of Hemingford Abbots and Archdeacon of Huntingdon by Richard Sledge.

Young was 46 when he was appointed Bishop of Ripon and was the youngest bishop at the time. He served in this post from 1977 for 22 years. Although not specifically a representative of 'muscular Christianity', he was a keen amateur athlete and in 1989 completed the London Marathon in under four hours, raising £30,000 in sponsorship money for his diocesan appeal.

During his episcopacy, his other roles included chairing the Partnership for World Mission (1978–86), SPCK (1979–88), the Archbishop of Canterbury's Inter-Faith Consultants and the Church of England Board of Education. The first 'academy' in Leeds was named the David Young Community Academy in recognition of his concern for all aspects of education.

Young retired in 1999, having been diagnosed with bone marrow cancer, myeloma. He was appointed CBE in the 2000 New Year Honours. He and Jane settled in the Dales, where he died on 10 August 2008.

Richard Kitson Sledge, Rector (1978–89)

Patron: HM the Queen

Richard Sledge was born on 13 April 1930 and educated at Epsom College and Peterhouse, Cambridge. He proceeded BA in 1952 and MA in 1957. His ministerial training was at Ridley Hall, Cambridge. He was ordained deacon in 1954 and priest in 1955. After curacies at Emmanuel Church, Plymouth (1954–57) and St Stephen's, Exeter (1957–63), he was Vicar of Dronfield (1973–76) and then Team Rector (1977–78), being also Rural Dean of Chesterfield (1972–78).

Figure 68 Richard Sledge

Sledge was Rector of Hemingford Abbots (1978–89), holding the post jointly with that of Archdeacon of Huntingdon (1978–89). The latter became a full-time appointment from 1989 to 1996. During this time, he and Patricia continued to live in the Rectory. As he wrote in the *Parish Magazine*, 'It is convenient for my journeys to Peterborough, Ely, St Neots and any of the 92 churches or 44 rectories that are in the area. Also we are happy to live here!'[319]

Richard and Patricia moved to Brampton on his retirement in 1996. He continued as an Honorary Canon of Ely Cathedral (1978–99). During his retirement, he was also the Bishop's Domestic Chaplain (1996–99) and Diocesan Retirement Officer (1998–99).

[319] *Hemingford Abbots Parish Magazine*, May 1989

From Rector to Priest-in-charge

In 1989, the part-time rector's position, which was linked with the arch-deaconry, was changed to being a priest-in-charge, linked with another parish. Initially, this was Hemingford Grey, which was very different from Hemingford Abbots. The evangelical approach contrasted with the broad-church traditions at Hemingford Abbots. In the nineteenth century, the Oxford Movement had emphasized the catholic roots of the Church of England and had had an influence on many parishes in the land, especially in the decoration of churches and the forms of worship. Some parishes, including Hemingford Abbots, adopted aspects of this, such as the use of Eucharistic vestments and lights on the altar, while steering a middle course theologically and ceremonially between high and low church.

From 1989 to 1996, Stephen Talbot was Priest-in-Charge of both Hemingfords. He resigned from Hemingford Abbots in 1996, and after a gap of a couple of years, Dorothy Wilman was appointed to Hemingford Abbots and Houghton-cum-Wyton. She retired four years later, and during another inter-regnum of two years, Ann Scott was a significant support as a Lay Minister. Further assistance was given by the Revs Peter Cameron, Ivan Weston, and Jeremy Craddock. Consideration was given in 2003 to developing links between the parishes of Fenstanton, Godmanchester, Hemingford Abbots, Hemingford Grey, and Hilton.[320] Impetus declined with the departure of Peter Moger, Vicar of Godmanchester from 2001 to 2010, to become Canon Precentor of York Minster.

In 2004, Peter Cunliffe, the Vicar of Hemingford Grey, was appointed Priest-in-Charge of Hemingford Abbots. He supported the training for ordination of Jon Randall and Judith Bolton, and each played a significant role in the parish. Several others have served as lay ministers, notably Gerald Barrett, Liz Pinnock, and Trish Latimer. Janine Hamilton has led the monthly family service for many years. Retired clergy, George Thomas and Canon Brian Atling, have assisted by leading the fort-nightly 8:30 Holy Communion services. Canon Atling, a resident and

[320] The Diocesan initiative 'All Good Gifts' encouraged parishes to work together more closely so that resources and specialities could be shared to meet needs more effectively. (Notes of meeting, 29 Sept 2003). The existing musical links were valued.

former churchwarden of the parish before being ordained in 2002, became formally linked with this parish in 2019, after retiring from the responsibilities of being Rural Dean, and has continued to play a significant role in the parish.

Clergy and lay ministers from Hemingford Grey have adapted to the style of worship while leading services at St Margaret's. Collaboration in the regatta since 1904 and the joint sports field and pavilion since the 1950s have encouraged a sense of community in the two villages, especially since the closures of the shop, post office, and primary school in Hemingford Abbots. The development of the pavilion, the Reading Room and the Parish Centre in Hemingford Grey and the replacement of Hemingford Abbots Village Hall in this century have led to an increase in activities supported by both villages. While the churchmanship continues to differ in emphasis, this increasingly has been valued as providing a wider range of worship opportunities for residents of both parishes. Several residents of Hemingford Grey and other villages support St Margaret's—including the choir, bellringers, Flower Guild, flower festivals, and carol services. A significant proportion of members on the electoral roll live outside the parish.

As well as the churchmanship, there are other differences and similarities between the two adjacent Hemingfords. For example, the population of Hemingford Grey in 2022 is about six times more than that of Hemingford Abbots (3654 vs 634), with almost double the density (2591 vs 1321 per square kilometre). The age profile of Hemingford Abbots is older, with 17% under 19 and 28% over 70, compared with Hemingford Grey's 21% under 19 and 22% over 70. Neighbourhoods within the two villages vary, and many residents value the contributions that the two churches make to the quality of life in complementing each other and providing choices in styles of Anglican worship.

While this account has deliberately focused on past rectors rather than recent clergy, it is appropriate to recognize the achievements of Peter Cunliffe, who has facilitated the range of services in the two parishes and established an effective parish office with staff and equipment that have supported these activities. Each incumbent has faced a variety of challenges. It is encouraging that St Margaret's continues to have both a regular congregation and attracts good support from others for special occasions.

Conclusions

Having investigated all the clergy for whom there are records, from approximately 1200 to 2021, a period of over 820 years, we can list the following statistics. Prior to the Reformation, thirty priests or incumbents are recorded, about most of whom little is known. Only a handful rose to any prominence. Although Weale notes that Ramsey Abbey continued its practice of 'presenting their livings to notable clerks',[321] only Michael Ravendale, Lawrence Booth, and Robert Bellamy were of national importance. Whether there were assistant clergy during this period is unknown.

In the post-Reformation period, a number of prominent clergymen held the post of rector, between John London and David Young. Two rectors have been raised to the episcopacy, one pre-Reformation (Lawrence Booth, Bishop of Durham, 1448), the other of much more recent memory (David Young, Bishop of Ripon, 1977). Like John London, several had important university connections, and in the early period after the Reformation, the parish was 'blessed with scholars'.[322]

A total of thirty-four rectors are recorded, twenty curates (though there were many besides these who have disappeared from the records), three deacons, and one preacher. There is some overlap in the posts. If we add the pre-Reformation clergy to the post-Reformation rectors, we arrive at sixty-four parsons, giving an average incumbency time of roughly 12.5 years. For the post-Reformation clergy, the figure is 13.7 years. Actual periods of incumbency varied widely, from a few months to over forty years.[323] Amongst the shortest were: Thomas Thompson (1555), Peter Heylin (1631), Theodore Crowley (1632), Alexander Burrell (1714), and David Young (1977), all of whom were in post for less than a year. At the other end of the scale, three served for over forty years: Charles Dickens (1748–93), 45 years; Henry Herbert (1867–1911), 44 years; and Arthur Yeldard, (1556–99), 43 years. The next longest-serving

---

[321] Colin Alexander Weale, 'Patronage Priest and Parish in the Archdeaconry of Huntingdon 1109-1547' (unpublished PhD dissertation, Middlesex University, 1996), p. 69. https://eprints.mdx.ac.uk/13500/ [accessed 15 October 2021].

[322] Weale, p. 69.

[323] The calculations are based on full years, disregarding the precise dates of incumbency, since these are not known in some cases.

were: Simeon Paige (1632–69), 37 years; Samuel Dickens (1714–48), 34 years; Edward Selwyn (1838–67), 29 years; and Archibald Obins (1811–38), 27 years. The longest-serving since 1900 were: Ernest Bawtree (1961–76), 15 years; Francis Herbert (1911–25), 14 years; Richard Sledge (1978–89), 11 years; Robert Balleine (1936–46), 10 years; and Priest-in-Charge Peter Cunliffe (2004–22), 18 years.

The ancient universities are fairly equally balanced. Sixteen rectors studied as undergraduates at Cambridge and fifteen at Oxford. Some proceeded to higher degrees, including BCL, BD, and DD. Early post-Reformation incumbents had sometimes been fellows of a college; a few were masters of a college. One was a graduate of Durham, and one had been ordained as part of his missionary work, without reading for a degree. There were several prebendaries and canons of cathedrals, and archdeacons. These were mainly incumbents who held parishes in plurality.

The various patrons clearly favoured certain types of incumbents. Most put their own relatives and friends into the living, e.g., Brooke, Paige, Bernard, Bernard Sparrow, and Herbert. Some incumbents were of aristocratic ancestry, while others had clear military connections. The troubled seventeenth century saw sequestrations and reversals of fortune, though Hemingford Abbots was less severely affected than many parishes. The eighteenth century saw a crop of typical country parsons, whereas the nineteenth brought some earnest and committed clergymen. Some patrons, such as Lady Olivia Bernard Sparrow, favoured staunchly Anglican, traditional Low-Church clergy, whereas others, such as the Herberts, were latitudinarians, possibly tending slightly towards the High-Church end. It is clear that the Herbert family set the direction of the parish for over 100 years from 1867 to 1976, which has been the foundation for its present-day complexion. As mentioned elsewhere, parish reorganizations, the accommodation of archdeacons, and the shift to part-time priests-in-charge have weakened the position of the patron and have led to much greater diocesan influence.

The parish of Hemingford Abbots is now at a turning-point, brought about by various factors. These include the retirement of the priest-in-charge in 2022, the effects of the Covid-19 pandemic, which has occasioned different forms of worship, including socially distanced congregations and online services and prayers from both Hemingford parishes, which attracted people from a wider area.

Figure 69 St Margaret's church in late 2021

Glossary of Terms[324]

Advowson
The right of appointing an incumbent to a parish or other ecclesiastical benefice.

BA
Bachelor of Arts (the first degree in any subject at Oxford and Cambridge)

BCL
Bachelor of Civil Law

BD
Bachelor of Divinity (a higher degree)

Benefice
A term originally used for a grant of land for life as a reward for services, in canon law it came to imply an ecclesiastical office which prescribed certain duties or conditions for the due discharge of which it provided certain revenues.

Canon
The clergy of a cathedral or collegiate church.

Chancel
Originally the part of the church immediately about the altar, now called the 'sanctuary'. When further space was reserved for clergy and choir westward from the sanctuary, the word was applied to this area as well and hence now normally designates the whole area in the main body of the church east of the nave and transepts.

Churchwarden
In the Church of England, churchwardens (usually two) are chosen annually by the incumbent and parishioners. They represent the laity and are responsible for the movable property in the church.

---

[324] Definitions are adapted from E. A. Livingstone, ed., *The Concise Oxford Dictionary of the Christian Church*, (Oxford University Press, 2014). A useful reference list is also to be found in the CCEd https://theclergydatabase.org.uk/reference/glossary/.

Commoner
See *pensioner*.

Curate
In general speech, … the word now denotes an assistant or unbeneficed cleric, i.e., one appointed to assist the incumbent, or to take charge of a parish temporarily during a vacancy or while the incumbent is incapacitated ('curate in charge'). Assistant curates are nominated by the incumbent or the bishop and licensed by the bishop.

DD
Doctor of Divinity (the highest-ranking degree)

Exhibitioner
A student at university in receipt of an exhibition. An exhibition at an Oxbridge college was the lower award. An exhibitioner received less money than a scholar, q.v.

Glebe
The land devoted to the maintenance of the incumbent of the parish. The term now excludes the parsonage house and the land occupied with it. In 1978 ownership of glebe land in England was transferred from the incumbent to the Diocesan Board of Finance.

Incumbent
In the Church of England the holder of a parochial benefice, i.e., a rector, vicar, (until 1969) a perpetual curate and (since 1969) a team rector.

Liber Cleri
Lists of clergy (incumbents, curates, readers, and preachers) and others (schoolmasters, churchwardens, and sometimes, surgeons and midwives) drawn up in advance of a visitation by an archdeacon, bishop or archbishop, or their officials.[325]

MA
Master of Arts (awarded to BAs upon seniority at Oxford and Cambridge, usually six years after the end of the first term of residence without further examination)

---

[325] https://theclergydatabase.org.uk/glossary/liber-cleri/

Parish
In England, an area under the spiritual care of a C of E priest (the incumbent), to whose religious ministrations all the inhabitants are entitled.

Parson
Properly, the holder of an ecclesiastical benefice who has full possession of its rights, i.e. a rector. This use was general until the 17th cent. The current use for any (especially C of E) cleric has superseded the original sense.

Patron of a benefice
The person or body that has right of appointing an incumbent to a parish or other ecclesiastical benefice.

Pensioner
At Cambridge University, also known as a *commoner*. A student who paid for his own lodging, tuition, and commons, i.e., meals.

Perpetual curate
In the C of E the technical name given before 1969 to a clergyman who officiated in a parish or district to which he had been nominated by the impropriator and licensed by the bishop. He received a stipend and had no right to tithes.

Prebendary
The title of the holder of a (now normally honorary) cathedral benefice. In the Middle Ages the endowment of most non-monastic cathedrals was divided into separate portions, known as 'prebends', each designed for the support of a single member of the chapter, and their holders became known as 'prebendaries'.

Priest-in-charge
In the C of E, a priest entrusted with the spiritual care of a parish under bishop's licence, where the patron's right of presentation was suspended under the Pastoral Measure 1983.

Rector
In the C of E, originally the person or body having the right to receive the whole tithes, at first always the incumbent.

Scholar
A student at university in receipt of a scholarship. A scholarship at an

Oxbridge college was the highest award; a scholar received more money and privileges than an exhibitioner, q.v.

Sizar

A poor undergraduate who received assistance with meals, fees, and lodgings, sometimes in return for doing a job in college.

Tithe

The tenth part of all fruits and profits due to God and thus to the Church for the maintenance of its ministry.

Vicar

In the Church of England, every incumbent is now either a rector or a vicar. Originally all were rectors. In medieval times, the tithes of a parish were often appropriated to other bodies, such as monasteries, who were then obliged to appoint and endow a vicar (or substitute) to perform the parochial duties. Today, in the C of E, as parish priest a vicar holds the same status as a rector.

Bibliography

Alumni Oxonienses: The Members of the University of Oxford, 1500–1714: Their Parentage Birthplace, and Year of Birth, with a Record of Their Degrees / (Oxford, 1891) http://hdl.handle.net/2027/pst.000007713354

Alumni Oxonienses: The Members of the University of Oxford, 1715–1886: Their Parentage, Birthplace, and Year of Birth, with a Record of Their Degrees / (Oxford, 1887) http://hdl.handle.net/2027/pst.000007713293

Arkell, T., 'Identifying Regional Variations from the Hearth Tax', *The Local Historian*, 33, no. 3 (August 2003)

Balleine, Robert, 'In Olden Days', *Hemingford Abbots Parish Magazine*, c. 1937

Barnard, John, *Theologo-Historicus, Or, The True Life of the Most Reverend Divine and Excellent Historian Peter Heylyn, D.D., Sub-Dean of Westminster: Also an Answer to Mr. Baxters False Accusations of Dr. Heylyn* (London: Printed for J.S. and are to be sold by Ed. Eckelston ..., 1683)

Barnes, Joshua, *The History of That Most Victorious Monarch, Edward IIId, King of England and France, and Lord of Ireland, and First Founder of the Most Noble Order of the Garter: Being a Full and Exact Account of the Life and Death of the Said King: Together with That of His Most Renowned Son, Edward, Prince of Wales and of Aquitain, Sirnamed the Black-Prince: Faithfully and Carefully Collected from the Best and Most Antient Authors, Domestick and Foreign, Printed Books, Manuscripts and Records* (Cambridge: Printed by John Hayes for the author, 1688)

Beresford, Charles and David Peace, *Hemingford Abbots Church: A Tour* (Hemingford Abbots, 2000, revised edition, 2007)

Beresford, Charles and Richard Butterfield, *Hemingford Abbots: Outline of a Village Story in its National Context* (Hemingford Abbots, 1995, second edition, 2015)

Beresford, Charles, *Angel Roof Carvings at St Margaret's Church, Hemingford Abbots* (Hemingford Abbots, 2017)

Beresford, Douglas K. and Brian K. Beresford, *The House of Beresford*, vol. 1, 1227–1727 (Beresford Family Society, 2011)

Birch, John and Roy Waight, 'Old Julius', p. 159. https://www.farnham-museumsociety.org.uk/Old_Julius.htm

Bradford, Charles Angell, *Helena, Marchioness of Northampton* (London: Allen & Unwin, 1936)

Broad, John, ed., *Bishop Wake's Summary of Visitation Returns from the Diocese of Lincoln 1706–15*, Part 2: *Huntingdonshire, Hertfordshire (Part), Bedfordshire, Leicestershire, Buckinghamshire, Records of Social and Economic History* (Oxford, New York: Oxford University Press, 2013)

Brooke, Samuel, *De Natura & Ordine divinae Praedestinationis in Ecclesia, vel intra Ecclesiam Dei.* Trinity College Cambridge MS B.15.13.

Brown, Bateman, *Reminiscences of Bateman Brown, J.P., A Collection of Articles First Published in 1895–96* (Peterborough Advertiser Company, Peterborough, 1905) https://www.cantab.net/users/michael.behrend/repubs/brown_reminisc/pages/index.html

'Potto Brown, Lady Olivia Sparrow, and William Loftie of Tandragee', Pottoingaround, 2013 https://pottoingaround.wordpress.com/2013/07/06/potto-brown-lady-olivia-sparrow-and-william-loftie-of-tandragee/

Brown, Susan, Judy Neiswander, Tim Ayers, Howard Cole and Steven Cole, *The Stained Glass Museum Gallery Guide* (Ely: The Stained Glass Museum, 2004)

Butterfield, Richard, 'All Aboard the Time Machine for a Thousand-Year Trip', *Hunts Post*, 2 May 1974, p. 4

Cambridge Alumni Database, https://venn.lib.cam.ac.uk/

Cartwright, J. L., *The Pictorial History of Peterborough Cathedral: Cathedral Church of St. Peter, St. Paul and St. Andrew* (London: Pitkin Pictorials, 1966)

Cherniavsky, Michael T., 'Joshua Barnes Historian', in: *7 Short Pieces* (privately printed, 1984)

Clay, Charles, 'Master Aristotle', *English Historical Review*, 76, No. 299 (April 1961), 303–08

Clemmow, Simon, 'Dissent in Post-Restoration Huntingdonshire', in: Evelyn Lord, ed., *The Singing Milkmaids: Life in Post-Restoration Huntingdonshire c.1660–c.1750* (Cambridge: EAH Press, 2019)

Clergy of the Church of England Database 1540–1835 (CCEd), https://theclergydatabase.org.uk/

Crockett, Alasdair and K. D. M. Snell, 'From the 1676 Compton Census to the 1851 Census of Religious Worship: Religious Continuity or Discontinuity?', *Rural History*, 8.1 (1997), 55–89

Crockford's Clerical Directory, 1865, 1932, and 2004 editions

Dady, Jack, *Beyond Yesterday: A History of Fenstanton*, Millennium edition (Fenstanton: Archival Books, 2002)

Darby, H. C., 'The Human Geography of the Fenland before the Drainage', *The Geographical Journal*, 80.5 (1932), https://doi.org/10.2307/1784229

Davies, R. Trevor, *Documents Illustrating the History of Civilization in Medieval England (1066–1500)* (New York: Barnes & Noble, 1969)

Day, Stephen, *Stained Glass in Huntingdonshire: A Field Guide: An Exploration of the Figurative Stained Glass Windows in the Anglican Parish Churches of Huntingdonshire* (Crawley & Crawley, 2018)

Dean, H. W., *Life's Survey: My Working Life*, ed. Charles Beresford (privately printed, 1993)

Dodgson, John McNeal, 'The Significance of the Distribution of the English Place-Name in *-ingas, -inga-* in South-East England', *Medieval Archaeology*, 10.1 (1966), 1–29 https://doi.org/10.1080/00766097.1966.11735279

Dorman, Bernard E., *The Story of Ely and its Cathedral* (Norwich: B.E. Dorman, 1968)

Dunn, Chris, Article on William Dowsing in: *Cambridgeshire Life*, February 2002, pp. 47–49

Edgington, Susan, trans., *Ramsey Abbey's Book of Benefactors* (Great Britain: Hakedes, 2001)

England & Wales, Prerogative Court of Canterbury Wills, 1384–1858

Fairbairn, James, *Fairbairn's Book of Crests of the Families of Great Britain and Ireland* (London: T. C. & E. C. Jack, 1905) http://archive.org/details/fairbairnsbookof01fair

Fairweather, Janet, trans., *Liber Eliensis: A History of the Isle of Ely from the Seventh Century to the Twelfth* (Woodbridge: The Boydell press, 2005)

Farnham Museum Society, 'To the Vicarage Born'.

Flanagan, Bridget, *A Story of Village Rowing: Hemingfords' Regatta 1901–2001* (Hemingford Grey: Bridget Flanagan, 2001)

Flanagan, Bridget, *Artists along the Ouse 1880–1930* (2010)

Ford, Liz, 'The Clergy in Post-Restoration Huntingdonshire and the Hearth Tax', in: Evelyn Lord, ed., *The Singing Milkmaids: Life in Post-Restoration Huntingdonshire c.1660–c.1750* (Cambridge: EAH Press, 2019)

Foster, Joseph, *Index Ecclesiasticus, or, Alphabetical Lists of All Ecclesiastical Dignitaries in England and Wales since the Reformation ...* (Oxford: Parker & Co., 1890)

Franklin, William, 'Huntingdonshire Fields c. 1660–c. 1750', in: Evelyn Lord, ed., *The Singing Milkmaids: Life in Post-Restoration Huntingdonshire c.1660–c.1750* (Cambridge: EAH Press, 2019)

Friar, Stephen, *A Companion to the English Parish Church* (Godalming, Surrey: Bramley Books, 1998)

Gaunt, Peter and Cromwell Association, *The Cromwellian Gazeteer: An Illustrated Guide to Britain in the Civil War and Commonwealth* (Stroud: Alan Sutton, 1992)

The Gentleman's Magazine, lxiii (2) (F. Jeffries, 1793) https://books.google.co.uk/books?id=PqY2AQAAMAAJ, p. 959

Goodman, Neville, C. P. Tebbutt, R. W. Dixon, and H. Allon, *Potto Brown: The Village Philanthropist* [Four Essays] (St Ives: A. Goodman, 1878) https://books.google.co.uk/books?id=_9H2VLU8R6oC

Gray, Adrian, *Restless Souls: Pilgrim Roots: The Turbulent History of Christianity in Nottinghamshire and Lincolnshire* (Retford: Bookworm, 2020)

Hart, Edward LeRoy, *Mormon in Motion: The Life and Journals of James H. Hurl, 1825–1906, in England, France, and America* (Utah: Windsor Books, 1978)

Hart, William Henry and Ponsonby A. Lyons, eds., *Cartularium Monasterii de Rameseia*, Cambridge Library Collection – Rolls (Cambridge: Cambridge University Press, 2012), vol. II https://doi.org/10.1017/CBO9781139380614

Hartley, J., *Craven Herald*, 3 August 1934

Hatcher, John, *Plague, Population and the English Economy, 1348–1530*, Studies in Economic and Social History (Cambridge: Economic History Society; distributed by Humanities Press, Atlantic Highlands, N.J. 1978)

Hearth Tax Digital: Huntingdonshire (forthcoming). https://www.roehampton.ac.uk/Research-Centres/Centre-for-Hearth-Tax-Research/.

Herbert, Nicholas [Lord Hemingford], 'A Tribute to Canon Ernest Anderson Bawtree', *Hemingford Abbots Parish Magazine*, February 1989 and *Scallop*, Hemingford Grey Parish Magazine, March 1989

Herbert, Nicholas [Lord Hemingford], *Successive Journeys: A Family in Four Continents* (Gamlingay: Authors OnLine, 2008)

Hodgett, G., *Tudor Lincolnshire* (Lincoln, 1975)

Huntingdonshire District Council, 'The Hemingfords Conservation Area June 2008 Character Assessment', https://www.huntingdonshire.gov.uk/media/2326/hemingfords-ca-character-assessment-adopted-june-2008.pdf

Kirby, Tony and Susan Oosthuizen, eds., *An Atlas of Cambridgeshire and Huntingdonshire History* (Cambridge: Centre for Regional Studies, Anglia Polytechnic University, 2000)

Lord, Evelyn, ed., *The Singing Milkmaids: Life in Post-Restoration Huntingdonshire c.1660–c.1750* (Cambridge: EAH Press, 2019)

Lutton, S. C., 'County Armagh Yeomanry', Review, *Journal of Craigavon Historical Society*, Vol. 1 No. 2 (1970) https://www.craigavonhistoricalsociety.org.uk/rev/luttonyeomanry.php

Lyons, Alice, *EAA 170: Rectory Farm, Godmanchester, Cambridgeshire: Excavations 1988–95, Neolithic Monument to Roman Villa Farm* (Cambridge: East Anglian Archaeology, 2020)

Macray, W.D., ed., *Chronicon Abbatiae Rameseiensis: A Saec. x. Usque Ad an. Circiter 1200: In Quatuor Partibus. Partes I., II., III., Iterum Post Th. Gale,*

Ex Chartulario in Archivis Regni Servato, Pars IV. Nunc Primum Ex Aliis Codicubus, Rerum Britannicarum Medii Aevi Scriptores, or, Chronicles and Memorials of Great Britain and Ireland during the Middle Ages (Longman, 1886) https://books.google.co.uk/books?id=-KgUAAAAQAAJ

Major, Kathleen, 'The Lincoln Diocesan Records', *Transactions of the Royal Historical Society* 22 (1940), 39–66, doi:10.2307/3678581

Malim, Tim, 'Neolithic Enclosures', no. 8, in: Tony Kirby and Susan Oosthuizen, *An Atlas of Cambridgeshire and Huntingdonshire History* (Cambridge: Centre for Regional Studies, Anglia Polytechnic University, 2000)

McCall, Fiona, *Baal's Priests: The Loyalist Clergy and the English Revolution* (London: Routledge, 2016)

McGoff-McCann, Michelle, *Melancholy Madness: A Coroner's Casebook* (Cork: Mercier, 2003)

Mills, A. D., *Hemingford Abbots*, in: *A Dictionary of English Place Names.* (Oxford: Oxford University Press, 2011)

Miscellany of Extracts from the Register, Vestry Book, and PCC Minutes, 1688–1950, compiled by several rectors of St Margaret's [manuscript, c. 1950, in private collection]

'Monumental Inscriptions in the Parish Church and Churchyard of St Margaret of Antioch', Hemingford Abbots, *Huntingdonshire Family History Society* 1991 (typescript).

Museum of the Manchester Regiment: The men behind the medals: Robert Balleine). http://www.themenbehindthemedals.org.uk/

Neilson, Nellie, 'Economic Conditions on the Manors of Ramsey Abbey', PhD Dissertation, Bryn Mawr College, Philadelphia, 1898 (Philadelphia: Sherman & Co., 1899)

Noble, William Mackreth, 'Incumbents of the County of Huntingdon', in *Transactions of the Cambridgeshire & Huntingdonshire Archaeological Society*, vol. III, pt IV (1910), 'Hemingford Abbots', pp. 119f.

Oman, Charles, *The Great Revolt of 1381* (London: Greenhill, 1989)

Oxford Dictionary of National Biography https://www.oxforddnb.com

Page, William, Granville Proby and H E Norris, 'Houses of Benedictine monks: The abbey of Ramsey,' in *A History of the County of Huntingdon: Volume 1*, ed. William Page, Granville Proby and H E Norris (London: Victoria County History, 1926), 377–385. *British History Online*, http://www.british-history.ac.uk/vch/hunts/vol1/pp377-385

Page, William, Granville Proby and S Inskip Ladds 'Parishes: Hemingford Abbots,' in *A History of the County of Huntingdon: Volume 2*, ed. William Page, Granville Proby and S Inskip Ladds (London: Victoria County History, 1932), 304–09. British History Online http://www.british-history.ac.uk/vch/hunts/vol2/pp304-309

Richard Parkinson, *General View of the Agriculture of the County of Huntingdon* (London: Printed for Sherwood, Neely, and Jones, 1813) http://books.google.com/books?id=fhNLAAAAYAAJ.

Peace, David, *The Engraved Glass of David Peace: The Architecture of Lettering* (Sheffield: Ruskin Gallery : Sheffield City Arts Department,1990)

'Peace, David Brian, (13 March 1915–15 Feb. 2003), Glass Engraver; Town Planner, 1947–82', 2007. *Who's Who 2021*, https://doi.org/10.1093/ww/9780199540884.013.U30334

[Petition] *To the Most Reverend Father in God, John Bird, Lord Archbishop of Canterbury ... We the Undersigned, Clergy of the United Church of England and Ireland, Etc. [An Address Directed against Certain Opinions Contained in "Essays and Reviews."]*, 1860 https://books.google.co.uk/books?id=Qu2-Z1uss0EC, p. 29

Pevsner, Nikolaus, *The Buildings of England: Bedfordshire and the County of Huntingdon and Peterborough* (Harmondsworth: Penguin Books, 1968)

Private Patrons' Advisory Group, Exercising Patronage in the Church of England (2000) https://www.clergyassoc.co.uk/content/docs/Patronage%20Guide.pdf

Raftis, J. A., *The Estates of Ramsey Abbey: A Study in Economic Growth and Organization*, Studies and Texts Pontifical Institute of Mediaeval Studies, 3 (Toronto: PIMS, 1957)

Raitt, Suzanne, *May Sinclair: A Modern Victorian* (Oxford: Clarendon Press, 2000).

Records of the Churches of Christ, Gathered at Fenstanton, Warboys, and Hex-ham, 1644–1720, edited for the Hanserd Knollys Society, by Edward Bean Underhill. (London: Printed for the Society, by Haddon Brothers, 1854)

'Reports and Papers of the Architectural and Archaeological Societies of the Counties of Lincoln and Northampton.', *Associated Architectural Societies' Reports and Papers,* vol. 16 (1891)

Richardson, Alan, 'The Tour of the Rev Timothy Neve DD through the Archdeaconry of Huntingdon May–July 1748', *Records of Huntingdonshire,* 2 (1987)

Richardson, Alan, *The Ecclesiastical Peculiars of Huntingdonshire, 1660–1852* (Huntingdon: Just Print IT!, 2007)

Royal Commission on Historical Monuments (England), An Inventory of the Historical Monuments in Huntingdonshire (London: H.M.S.O., 1926)

Sawyer, P.H., *Anglo-Saxon Charters* (London: Royal Historical Society, 1968)

Shaw, William Arthur, *A History of the English Church during the Civil Wars and under the Commonwealth, 1640–1660,* vol. 1 (London: Longmans, Green, and Co., 1900)

'Speculum Dioceseos Sub Episcopo Johanne Thomas A.D. 1744–61 | Lincs to the Past' https://www.lincstothepast.com/Speculum-Dioceseos-sub-episcopo-Johanne-Thomas-A-D--1744-61/722087.record?pt=S.

Spufford, Margaret, *Contrasting Communities: English Villages in the Sixteenth and Seventeenth Centuries* (Cambridge: Cambridge University Press, 1979)

Srawley, J. H, *The Story of Lincoln Minster, by J.H. Srawley. With a Foreword by the Dean of Lincoln.* (London: Raphael, Tuck, 1933)

Survey of English Place-Names: A county-by-county guide to the linguistic origins of England's place-names – a project of the English Place-Name Society, founded 1923. http://epns.nottingham.ac.uk/browse/Huntingdon-shire/Hemingford+Abbots+and+Grey/53282b41b47fc407a900035d-Hemingford.

Thomas of Ely, *Liber Eliensis, ad fidem codicum variorum.* Londini, Impensis Societatis, 1848), http://archive.org/details/libereliensisadf01thom

Thomas of Ely, *Liber Eliensis*, trans. by Janet Fairweather (Boydell Press, 2005)

Thomson, Oliver, *From the Bloody Heart: The Stewarts and the Douglases* (History Press, 2003)

Tyrrell-Green, Edmund, *Baptismal Fonts: Classified and Illustrated* by E. Tyrrell-Green, Historic Monuments of England (London: New York: Society for Promoting Christian Knowledge; Macmillan Co., 1928)

Vallance, Aymer, *English Church Screens* (Batsford, 1936)

Venn, J., *Alumni Cantabrigienses: A Biographical List of All Known Students, Graduates and Holders of Office at the University of Cambridge, from the Earliest Times to 1900*, Alumni Cantabrigienses 2 Volume Set (Cambridge University Press, 2011), superseded by *Cambridge Alumni Database*, https://venn.lib.cam.ac.uk/

Warton, Thomas, *The Life of Sir Thomas Pope, Founder of Trinity College, Oxford* (T. Davies, T. Becket, T. Walters, and J. Fletcher, 1772).

Weale, Colin Alexander, 'Patronage Priest and Parish in the Archdeaconry of Huntingdon 1109–1547' (PhD thesis, Middlesex University, 1996) https://eprints.mdx.ac.uk/13500/

Whiteman, Anne and Mary Clapinson, *The Compton Census of 1676: A Critical Edition*, Edited by Anne Whiteman with the Assistance of Mary Clapinson, *Records of Social and Economic History*; New Ser., 10 (London: Oxford University Press for the British Academy, 1986)

Whitley, W. T., *Minutes of the General Assembly of the General Baptist Churches in England: With Kindred Records*, Edited with Introduction and Notes for the Baptist Historical Society, by W. T. Whitley (London: Printed for the Society by the Kingsgate Press, 1909), vol. 1, 1654–1728

Wickes, Michael, *A History of Huntingdonshire* (Chichester: Phillimore, 1995)

Willis, Browne, *A Survey of the Cathedrals of York, Durham, Carlisle, Chester, Man, Litchfield, Hereford, Worcester, Gloucester, Bristol, Lincoln, Ely, Oxford, Peterborough, Canterbury, Rochester, London, Winchester, Chichester, Norwich, Bangor, and St. Asaph ...* (T. Osborne in Gray's Inn and T. Bacon in Dublin, 1742)

Wise, J. and W. M. Noble, *Ramsey Abbey: Its Rise and Fall* (Huntingdon: Edis & Cooper; Ramsey: Palmer & Son; London: Simpkin, Marshall & Co., 1881) https://books.google.co.uk/books?id=OQ0HAAAAQAAJ

Yates, Nigel, *Eighteenth Century Britain: Religion and Politics 1714–1815* (London: Routledge, 2014) https://doi.org/10.4324/9781315834979

Yeandle, David, 'Hemingford Abbots' School', http://www.hem-locs.co.uk/Abbotsschool.html

Yeandle, David, *A Victorian Curate: A Study of the Life and Career of the Rev. Dr John Hunt* (Cambridge, UK: Open Book Publishers, 2021) https://doi.org/10.11647/OBP.0248

Appendix

Abbots of Ramsey[326]

Name	Elected	Ceased	Died
Ædnoth	992	1008	
Wulsi	1008		1016
Wythman	1016	1020	
Ethelstan	1020		1043
Alfwin	1043	1080	
Ailsi	1080	1087	
Herbert of Lorraine	1087	1091	
Aldwin	1091		1113
Bernard of St. Albans	1102		1107
Reynold	1114		1133
Walter	1133		1161
William	1161	1177	
Robert Trianel	1180		1200
Eudo	1200	1202	
Robert de Reading	1202	1207	
Richard de Selby	1214	1216	
Hugh Foliot	1216		1231
Ranulf	1231		1253
William de Hacholt or Akolt	1253		1254
Hugh de Sulgrave	1254		1267
William de Godmanchester, sacristan	1267	1285	
John de Sawtry	1285		1316

[326] 'Houses of Benedictine monks: The abbey of Ramsey,' in *A History of the County of Huntingdon: Volume 1*, ed. William Page, Granville Proby and H E Norris (London: Victoria County History, 1926), pp. 377–85. *British History Online*, accessed July 7, 2021, http://www.british-history.ac.uk/vch/hunts/vol1/pp377-385.

Simon de Eye	1316	1343
Robert de Nassington	1343	1349
Richard de Sheningdon	1349	1379
Edmund de Ellington	1379	1396
Thomas Butterwick	1396	1419
John Tichmersh	1419	1434
John Crowland	1434	1436
John Stow	1436	1468
William Wittlesey	1468	1473
John Wardboys	1473	1489
John Huntingdon	1489	
Henry Stukeley	1506	
John Lawrence, alias Wardboys	1507	

Domesday Book 1086 (Translation)[327]

In HEMINGFORD [Abbots] the Abbot of Ramsey had 18 hides taxable. Land for 16 ploughs. Now in lordship 2 ploughs; 26 villagers and 5 smallholders with 8 ploughs. A church and a priest. 1 mill, 10s 8d; meadow, 80 acres. Value before 1066 £11; now £10.

There also HEMINGFORD [Abbots] Godric the sheriff had 1 hide taxable. He held from the Abbot. Land for 1 plough. Now Ralph son of Osmund has it, but the men of the Hundred do not know through whom. Value before 1066, 10s; now 3s.

In another estate called HEMINGFORD are 5 hides taxable. Land for 5 ploughs. Jurisdiction in Hemingford [Abbots]. Now Aubrey de Vere has it from the Abbot and a man-at-arms has 2 hides of this land under him. In lordship 1 plough; 8 villagers with 3 ploughs. Meadow, 20 acres. Value before 1066 and now 60s. (*Domesday Book*, Folio 204v)[328]

[327] See https://www.1066.co.nz/Mosaic%20DVD/index.htm. For the original text and facsimiles, see https://opendomesday.org/place/TL2871/hemingford-abbots/.

[320] http://www.1066.co.nz/Mosaic%20DVD/library/domesday/Folio_204v_Huntingdonshire.html.

They testify that the lands of Aelfric the sheriff in YELLING and HEMINGFORD [Grey] were St Benedict's of Ramsey; and that they were granted to Aelfric for his lifetime on this condition that after his death they should have returned to the church, and Boxted with them. However Aelfric himself was killed in the battle at Hastings, and the Abbot recovered his lands, until Aubrey de Vere dispossessed him.

Concerning the 2 hides which Ralph son of Osmund holds in HEMINGFORD [Abbots], they say that one of them was part of the lordship of the Church of Ramsey in King Edward's day and that he holds it against the Abbot's will. Concerning the other hide, they say that Godric the sheriff held it from the Abbot, but when the Abbot was in Denmark, Ralph's father, Osmund, seized it from Saewin the falconer, to whom the Abbot had given it out of his love for the King. (*Domesday Book*, Folio 208, TOSELAND Hundred)[329]

In HEMINGFORD [Grey] Ordwy of Hemingford had 4 hides taxable. Land for 3 ploughs. (Folio 206 TOSELAND Hundred)[330]

In YELLING Aelfric the sheriff had 5 hides taxable. Land for 8 ploughs. Now in lordship 2 ploughs; 10 villagers and 2 smallholders with 3 ploughs. A church and a priest. Meadow, 40 acres; underwood, 5 acres. Value before 1066 and now £4.

In HEMINGFORD [Grey] Aelfric the sheriff had 11 hides taxable. Land for 7 ploughs. Now in lordship 2 ploughs; 13 villagers and 4 smallholders who have 5 ploughs. 2 mills, £6; a fishery, 6s; meadow, 50 acres. Value before 1066 and now £12. Aelfric held these two manors from the Abbot of Ramsey before 1066. Now Aubrey de Vere holds from the King, and Ralph son of Osmund from him. (The Land of Aubrey de Vere TOSELAND Hundred)

In HEMINGFORD [Abbots] Alwin Blaec had 1 hide taxable. Land for 1 plough. It is waste. Ralph son of Osmund has it. (The Land of Ralph son of Osmund TOSELAND Hundred)[331]

---

[329] http://www.1066.co.nz/Mosaic%20DVD/library/domesday/Folio_208_Huntingdonshire.html.

[330] http://www.1066.co.nz/Mosaic%20DVD/library/domesday/Folio_206_Huntingdonshire.html.

[331] http://www.1066.co.nz/Mosaic%20DVD/library/domesday/Folio_207_Huntingdonshire.html.

Pre-Reformation Clergy[332]

Name	Started	Finished	Died
Aristotle	c. 1199?		
R(obert) Morell	1218		
John Clarel	1251		1295
Robert de Sautre	1295		
John			1312
Robert Hunter de Abyngdon	1312	1314	
Hugh Sampson	1314		1334
Ivo (John) de Sappy	1334		
Robert de Spaldingh[333]	1336 (?)	1344	
John Edward	1344		
Thomas Cok		1361	
Robert de Swinfen	1361	1361	1361
Michael de Ravensdale[334]	1361	1373	
John de Ratforde	1373		
John Wade de Bratyngthorpe[335]	1378	1385	
Thomas Jewelston	1385	1386	
William Buckingham	1386	1404	
Richard Warwyk	1404	1406	
Robert Wytleseye	1406	1412	
Thomas Tybary	1412	1419	1419

[332] The patron for all appointments except John Wade was the Abbot and Monastery of Ramsey.

[333] 'Under date 20th March, 1336–7, we find "Ratification of the Estate of Master Rob. de Spaldyngh as parson of the church of Abbots Hemmingford, notwithstanding any right of the King therein by reason of the Abbey of Ramsey or the temporalities thereof being in the hands of the King." He was still Rector in 1344, in which year John Edward is also mentioned as Rector.' Noble, p. 119, fn. 5.

[334] Noble gives the name as Ravensdale, but Ravendale is normal. Weale notes (p. 69): 'Evidently, the abbey continued its practice of presenting their livings to notable clerks, as on 19 September, 1361 Michael Ravendale, a clerk in chancery, was instituted to the church of Hemingford Abbots, in its gift. He succeeded M. Robert de Swinfen who had died.'

[335] Patron: King Richard II, Ramsey Abbey being void.

John Estheton	1419	1420	
William Ryley	1420	1422	
Edmund Nicholl	1422		
Thomas Pulter		1444	
Lawrence Booth/Bothe	1444	1448	
William Fraunceys	1448	1455	
Edmund Shireff/Argenten	1455	1476	
Robert Bel[l]amy	1476	1492	1492
Edmund Hanson	1492	1512	1512
Lewes Williams	1513	1524	1524

Post-Reformation Clergy[336]

Date Order

Standardized Name	Date	Event	Post	CCEd
London, John	1540	Libc	Rector	84433
Mane, John	1540	Libc	Curate	148318
Lego, Percival	1544	Appt	Rector	147959
London, John	1544	Death	Rector	84433
Thompson, Thomas	1555	Present	Rector	-
Unknown	1555	Death	Rector	-
Yeldard, Arthur	1556	Present	Rector	8364
Ford, Anthony	1572	Libc	Curate	144197
Yeldard, Nicholas	1573	Libc	Curate	154529
Mariat, Henry	1574	Libc	Curate	148398
Mariat, Henry	1578	Libc	Curate	148398
Lewes, Christopher	1585	Libc	Curate	148010
Yeldard, Arthur	1585	Libc	Rector	8364
Price, Humphrey	1591	Libc	Curate	150471

[336] Most of the details are taken from *The Clergy of the Church of England Database 1540–1835* (CCEd). The final column records a number for each clergyman. https://theclergydatabase.org.uk/. Key to abbreviations: Disp 'Dispensation'; Instit 'Institution'; Appt 'Appointment; Libc 'Liber Cleri' of Lincoln Diocese; Licens 'Licensing'; Resig 'Resignation'; Subsc 'Subscription'; Present 'Presentation'; St Curate 'Stipendiary Curate'.

Cooke, George	1597	Libc	Curate	142521
Yeldard, Arthur	1597	Libc	Rector	8364
Shaxton, John	1598	Instit	Rector	151447
Cooke, George	1599	Libc	Curate	142521
Chamberlen, Barth.	1600	Instit	Rector	2313
Chamberlen, Barth.	1614	Libc	Rector	2313
Brooke, Samuel	1622	Disp	Rector	25055
Brooke, Samuel	1622	Instit	Rector	25055
Crowley, Theodore	1631	Disp	Rector	40158
Heylin, Peter	1631	Present	Rector	107125
Crowley, Theodore	1632	Resig	Rector	40158
Crowley, Theodore	1632	Instit	Rector	40158
Paige, Simeon	1632	Instit	Rector	100643
Paige, Simeon	1662	Subsc	Rector	100643
Edmonds, Thomas	1669	Instit	Rector	88074
Paige, Simeon	1669	Death	Rector	100643
Rowley, John	1669	Subsc	Rector	102190
Slater, John	1680	Licens	Curate	103079
Dickens, William	1687	Licens	Preacher	14895
Hanbury, Robert	1688	Licens	Preacher	7200
Hanbury, Robert	1688	Instit	Rector	7200
Rowley, John	1688	Death	Rector	102190
Whishaw, Thomas	1709	Licens	Curate	80008
Hanbury, Robert	1712	Death	Rector	7200
Smith, John	1712	Instit	Rector	105450
Dicken, Samuel	1713	Licens	Deacon	13203
Dicken, Samuel	1714	Instit	Rector	13203
Smith, John	1714	Death	Rector	105450
Barber, George	1727	Licens	Deacon	86026
Nicholls, Henry	1731	Licens	Deacon	100554
Williamson, John	1732	Licens	Deacon	105060
Pawlett, Charles	1739	Licens	Curate	72122
Dickens, Charles	1744	Licens	Curate	10607
Dicken, Samuel	1748	Death	Rector	13203
Dickens, Charles	1748	Instit	Rector	10607
Filewood, Thomas Roger	1769	Licens	Curate	59482

Hopkins, John	1780	Licens	Curate	64997
Ayerst, William Gunsley	1781	Licens	Curate	1556
Cowling, William	1789	Licens	Curate	53726
Dickens, Charles	1793	Death	Rector	10607
Stafford, Thomas	1793	Disp	Rector	76863
Stafford, Thomas	1793	Instit	Rector	76863
Greene, Charles	1797	Instit	Rector	61536
Stafford, Thomas	1797	Death	Rector	76863
Greene, Charles	1803	Death	Rector	61536
Pery, John	1803	Disp	Rector	2055
Pery, John	1803	Instit	Rector	2055
Obins, Archibald Eyre	1811	Instit	Rector	71664
Pery, John	1811	Death	Rector	2055
Buddell, John	1817	Appt	St Curate	-
Davies, Morgan	1818	Licens	St Curate	54615
Torlesse, Charles Martin	1821	Licens	St Curate	77639
Blackden	1823	Licens	St Curate	9468
Wilde, Ralph	1825	Licens	St Curate	80408
Davies, Henry Lewis	1834	Licens	St Curate	6699
Selwyn, Edward	1838	Licens	Rector	-
Herbert, Henry	1867	Licens	Rector	-
Herbert, Francis Falkner	1911	Licens	Rector	-
Frith, Hugh Cokayne	1925	Licens	Rector	-
George, Frank Henry	1926	Licens	Rector	-
Ayre, Algernon Early	1931	Licens	Rector	-
Clements, Julius	1932	Licens	Rector	-
Balleine, Robert Wilfred	1936	Licens	Rector	-
Denison, Herbert	1946	Licens	Rector	-
Stevens, James Reginald	1955	Licens	Rector	-
Bawtree, Ernest Anderson	1961	Licens	Rector	-
Young, David Nigel de L.	1977	Licens	Rector	-
Sledge, Richard Kitson	1978	Licens	Rector	-

Name Order

Standardized Name	Date	Event	Post	CCEd
Ayerst, William Gunsley	1781	Licens	Curate	1556
Ayre, Algernon Early	1931	Licens	Rector	-
Balleine, Robert Wilfred	1936	Licens	Rector	-
Barber, George	1727	Licens	Deacon	86026
Bawtree, Ernest Anderson	1961	Licens	Rector	-
Blackden	1823	Licens	St Curate	9468
Brooke, Samuel	1622	Disp	Rector	25055
Brooke, Samuel	1622	Instit	Rector	25055
Buddell, John	1817	Appt	St Curate	-
Chamberlen, Barth.	1600	Instit	Rector	2313
Chamberlen, Barth.	1614	Libc	Rector	2313
Clements, Julius	1932	Licens	Rector	-
Cooke, George	1597	Libc	Curate	142521
Cooke, George	1599	Libc	Curate	142521
Cowling, William	1789	Licens	Curate	53726
Crowley, Theodore	1631	Disp	Rector	40158
Crowley, Theodore	1632	Resig	Rector	40158
Crowley, Theodore	1632	Instit	Rector	40158
Davies, Henry Lewis	1834	Licens	St Curate	6699
Davies, Morgan	1818	Licens	St Curate	54615
Denison, Herbert	1946	Licens	Rector	-
Dicken, Samuel	1713	Licens	Deacon	13203
Dicken, Samuel	1714	Instit	Rector	13203
Dicken, Samuel	1748	Death	Rector	13203
Dickens, Charles	1744	Licens	Curate	10607
Dickens, Charles	1748	Instit	Rector	10607
Dickens, Charles	1793	Death	Rector	10607
Dickens, William	1687	Licens	Preacher	14895
Edmonds, Thomas	1669	Instit	Rector	88074
Filewood, Thomas Roger	1769	Licens	Curate	59482
Ford, Anthony	1572	Libc	Curate	144197
Frith, Hugh Cokayne	1925	Licens	Rector	-
George, Frank Henry	1926	Licens	Rector	-
Greene, Charles	1797	Instit	Rector	61536

Greene, Charles	1803	Death	Rector	61536
Hanbury, Robert	1688	Licens	Preacher	7200
Hanbury, Robert	1688	Instit	Rector	7200
Hanbury, Robert	1712	Death	Rector	7200
Herbert, Francis Falkner	1911	Licens	Rector	-
Herbert, Henry	1867	Licens	Rector	-
Heylin, Peter	1631	Present	Rector	107125
Hopkins, John	1780	Licens	Curate	64997
Lego, Percival	1544	Appt	Rector	147959
Lewes, Christopher	1585	Libc	Curate	148010
London, John	1540	Libc	Rector	84433
London, John	1544	Death	Rector	84433
Mane, John	1540	Libc	Curate	148318
Mariat, Henry	1574	Libc	Curate	148398
Mariat, Henry	1578	Libc	Curate	148398
Nicholls, Henry	1731	Licens	Deacon	100554
Obins, Archibald Eyre	1811	Instit	Rector	71664
Paige, Simeon	1632	Instit	Rector	100643
Paige, Simeon	1662	Subsc	Rector	100643
Paige, Simeon	1669	Death	Rector	100643
Pawlett, Charles	1739	Licens	Curate	72122
Pery, John	1803	Disp	Rector	2055
Pery, John	1803	Instit	Rector	2055
Pery, John	1811	Death	Rector	2055
Price, Humphrey	1591	Libc	Curate	150471
Rowley, John	1669	Subsc	Rector	102190
Rowley, John	1688	Death	Rector	102190
Selwyn, Edward	1838	Licens	Rector	-
Shaxton, John	1598	Instit	Rector	151447
Slater, John	1680	Licens	Curate	103079
Sledge, Richard Kitson	1978	Licens	Rector	-
Smith, John	1712	Instit	Rector	105450
Smith, John	1714	Death	Rector	105450
Stafford, Thomas	1793	Disp	Rector	76863
Stafford, Thomas	1793	Instit	Rector	76863
Stafford, Thomas	1797	Death	Rector	76863
Stevens, James Reginald	1955	Licens	Rector	-

Thompson, Thomas	1555	Present	Rector	-
Torlesse, Charles Martin	1821	Licens	St Curate	77639
Unknown	1555	Death	Rector	-
Whishaw, Thomas	1709	Licens	Curate	80008
Wilde, Ralph	1825	Licens	St Curate	80408
Williamson, John	1732	Licens	Deacon	105060
Yeldard, Arthur	1556	Present	Rector	8364
Yeldard, Arthur	1585	Libc	Rector	8364
Yeldard, Arthur	1597	Libc	Rector	8364
Yeldard, Nicholas	1573	Libc	Curate	154529
Young, David Nigel de L.	1977	Licens	Rector	-

Bishop Wake's Visitation Returns 1706, 1709 and 1712[337]

[Hemmingford Abbots HNT/046] Hemingford-Abbats (page 76) Deanery St Neots
a) Mr Robert Hanbury AM Rector.
Sir John Bernard of Brampton, Huntingdonshire Patron.
b) The Parish is between 7 & 8 miles in Compasse; and has betwixt 50 and 60 families in it.
Of these three are Anabaptists: 3 Quakers: There is but One person a Presbyterian: Not one papist, or reputed papist in the Parish.
The Rectory is worth 150 per Annum.
There is no Lecture, School, Almeshouse or Hospital endow'd within this parish. No Charitie Schole.
No Person of Qualitie or Gentleman of Estate lives, or has his Seat in it.
There are no Monuments of note within the Church, Or Antiquities in the parish.
[Exhibit. in Visit. A.D 1706]

---

[337] John Broad, ed., *Bishop Wake's Summary of Visitation Returns from the Diocese of Lincoln 1706–15, Part 2: Huntingdonshire, Hertfordshire (Part), Bedfordshire, Leicestershire, Buckinghamshire*, Records of Social and Economic History (Oxford, New York: Oxford University Press, 2013), p. 536

178

[Visit. A.D. 1709]
a) Rector of Denton in Yaxley: qv Priested 20 September 1674. Instituted to this Living, November: Inducted 9 February 1688.
b) Families 60 Souls, 250. No Papist: Dissenters in all 21. The Anabaptists have a meeting here once a Month: Their Teacher One Clarke: Their number about 30.
Communicants about 60, Of these 30 usually receive. Yet not above 16 did communicate at Easter last.
One Mr Barely has left £13 [gap] to the parish for the poor.
Mr Thomas Wishaw Curate Priested 25 September 1709 William [bishop of] Lincoln. Licensed Curate 26 September.

[Visit. A.D. 1712][87]
Mr John Smyth AM Rector: Instituted 22 January 1711.
Families 61: of which 2 of Quakers: One of Anabaptists.
The Rector resides in his Parsonage House.
Divine Service twice every Lords day.
Catechizing promised to be duly performed.
Communion thrice a year. About 15 received at Easter last. Notice duly given.

[87] MS 273 1712 at end of return notes 2 adults baptized: Anne Marriott, Richard Beaumont.

The Authors and Consultant

The authors and consultant are all parishioners of Hemingford Abbots, who have known between six and eight of the most recent incumbents. They are Cambridge graduates, who have worked in Cambridge and London. They have served on the PCC and taken part in the biennial Flower Festival that raises funds for the maintenance and improvement of the church building by involving a significant proportion of residents.

Authors

Charles Beresford, MA (Cantab.), PhD (London), has lived in the Hemingfords since 1966. He has retired from being Principal Inspector of Staff Development in Cambridgeshire and Research Associate in strategies for school improvement at the Institute of Education in London University. He has served as Churchwarden and for twenty years as Choirmaster. He is also a Trustee of the Friends of St Margaret's and has served as a Flower Festival Chairman.

David Yeandle, MA, PhD (Cantab.), is the grandson and son of the former Head Teacher and Assistant Teacher at Hemingford Abbots Church of England School. He has lived in the Hemingfords intermittently since 1961. He has sung in St Margaret's Choir since he was a boy and has served as an occasional organist and choirmaster. He has served on the PCC and as an altar server and sidesman. He is Emeritus Professor of German at King's College, London University.

Consultant

Nicholas Herbert, MA (Cantab.), 3rd Lord Hemingford, is the great-grandson and great-nephew of two of the rectors. He succeeded his grandfather and father as Patron. His parents bought the Old Rectory when it was sold by the Diocese in 1949, and it continues to be owned by the family. He has retired from being Editorial Director of the Westminster Press and Chairman of the East Anglian Committee of the National Trust. He was Chairman of the Flower Festival Committee for several years, was the founder of the Friends of St Margaret's in 2004 and served as its chairman until 2019.

Printed in Great Britain
by Amazon

33717364R00109